T0338124

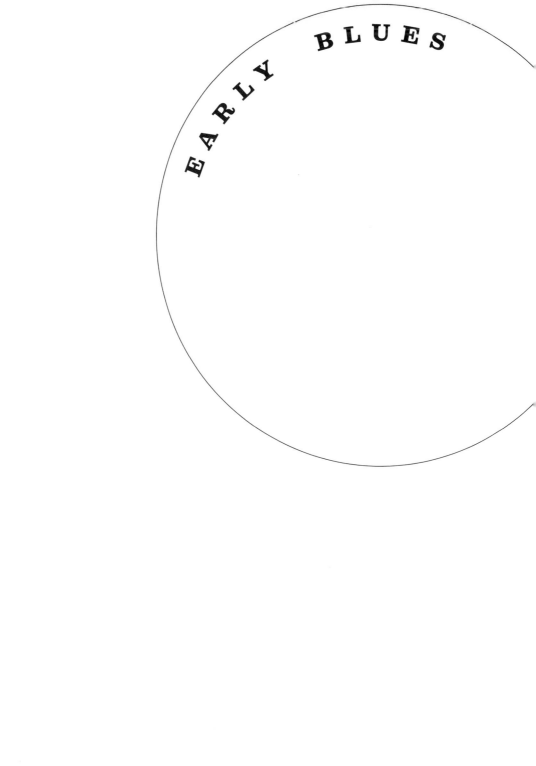

EARLY BLUES

EARLY BLUES

THE

FIRST STARS

OF BLUES

GUITAR

JAS OBRECHT

University of Minnesota Press

Minneapolis • London

Published by the University of Minnesota Press
111 Third Avenue South, Suite 290
Minneapolis, MN 55401-2520
http://www.upress.umn.edu

Library of Congress Cataloging-in-Publication Data
Obrecht, Jas.
Early blues : the first stars of blues guitar / Jas Obrecht.
Includes bibliographical references and index.
ISBN 978-0-8166-9804-2 (hc)
ISBN 978-0-8166-9805-9 (pb)
1. Blues (Music)—1921–1930—History and criticism. 2. Blues musicians—
United States. 3. Guitarists—United States. 4. Weaver, Sylvester.
5. Jackson, Papa Charlie. 6. Jefferson, Blind Lemon, 1897–1929.
7. McTell, Blind Willie. 8. Johnson, Blind Willie. 9. Johnson, Lonnie.
10. Hurt, Mississippi John, 1892–1966. 11. Tampa Red, 1904–1981. I. Title.
ML3521.O27 2015
787.87'1643092273—dc23   2015023632

Printed in the United States of America on acid-free paper

The University of Minnesota is an equal-opportunity educator and employer.

21 20 19 18 17 16 15   10 9 8 7 6 5 4 3 2 1

For Ava, with love

CONTENTS

Acknowledgments

FIRST AND FOREMOST, I would like to express my appreciation for the original artists profiled in these pages, as well as for the 78 collectors and record companies who have made their recordings available. How lucky we are to live in an era when the complete recorded works of nearly all of the prewar blues musicians are easily accessible. Special thanks to Johnny Parth of Document Records for sending me his CD catalog of prewar blues recordings and to Roger Misiewicz and Helge Thygesen for providing the book's 78 label artwork.

I owe a great debt of gratitude to the first wave of blues researchers and writers for their groundbreaking work, as well as for their contributions to this book. Primary among these are Samuel Charters and Paul Oliver, whose writings have inspired generations of blues writers. Mr. Charters graciously permitted me to quote his pioneering research into the lives of Papa Charlie Jackson, Blind Lemon Jefferson, Blind Willie Johnson, and Lonnie Johnson. Paul Oliver gave me audio copies of his original interviews with Lonnie Johnson, which I carefully retranscribed for this book. Chris Albertson, who managed Lonnie Johnson's career in the 1960s, added significant new insights. David Evans, the leading authority on Blind Willie McTell, offered access to his extensive interview materials related to McTell and fact-checked that chapter. Stefan Grossman, who has done much to keep 1920s guitar blues in the public eye, added shrewd observations to many parts of the book. Paramount Records expert Gayle Dean Wardlow shared his research and insight. Alan Balfour extended support and served as a liaison to the community of British blues scholars. Dick Waterman shared his memories and photographs of Mississippi John Hurt and other country bluesmen. Jim O'Neal, whose work as the founding editor of *Living Blues* magazine inspired me to become a music journalist, provided valuable assistance on many fronts.

The insights of many other writers, researchers, and collectors informed these pages: Mary Katherine Aldin, Dean Alger, Moses Asch, Scott Baretta, Bruce Bastin, Derrick Stewart Baxter, Jonathan Black, Matt Blackett, Pen Bogert, Brett Bonner, Toby Byron, Steve Calt, Larry Cohn, Michael Corcoran, Alan Di Perna, Bob Eagle, Anne Evans, Jim Ferguson, Bill Ferris, Richard Flohill, Dan Forte, David Fulmer, Paul Garon, John Goddard, Alan Govenar, Tim Gracyk, Michael Gray, Peter Guralnick, Steve Hoffman, Tom Hoskins, Paul Hostetter, Mark Humphrey, Edward Komara, Peter Lee, David Leishman, Alan Lomax, Thom Carlyle Loubet, Woody Mann, Mike Newton, Robert Palmer, Nick Perls, David Ritz, Mike Rowe, Tony Russell, James Sallis, John Sebastian, Robert Shelton, Victoria Spivey, Dick Spottswood, John Tefteller, Cheryl Thurber, Jeff Todd Titon, Steven C. Tracy, George Van Eps, Guido van Rijn, Dave Van Ronk, Amy van Singel, Hans Vergeer, Max Vreede, Dick Waterman, Pete Whelan, Valerie Wilmer, Bob Yelin, and the staffs of *78 Quarterly, Blues & Rhythm, Blues Access, Blues Unlimited, Guitar Player, Living Blues, Record Research, Sing Out!,* and *Victrola & 78 Journal.* I thank you all—and sincere apologies to anyone I missed.

Hats off to the performing artists who agreed to be interviewed for this book: Norman Blake, Rory Block, Ry Cooder, Blind John Davis, Stefan Grossman, John Hammond, John Lee Hooker, Steve James, Jorma Kaukonen, B.B. King, Dan Lambert, Nick Lucas, Country Joe McDonald, Johnny Shines, Pops Staples, and Johnny Winter. Special thanks to Billy Gibbons for making that pilgrimage to Indianapolis all those years ago to interview B.B. King with me.

Acting on Jim O'Neal's suggestion, I asked expert researcher and cutting-edge discographer Alex van der Tuuk to skim a few of the sections related to Paramount Records. Alex voluntarily went far deeper into the manuscript, updating session dates, personnel, song titles, locations, and, in many cases, biographical information. Thanks to Robert M. W. Dixon, John Godrich, and Howard Rye for their monumental reference book *Blues & Gospel Records, 1890–1943*; to Mike Leadbitter, Leslie Fancourt, Paul Pelletier, and Neil Slaven for *Blues Records, 1943–1970*; and to Guido van Rijn and Alex van der Tuuk for their *New York Recording Laboratories Matrix Series,* volumes 1–4. These books, completed as labors of love, are must-haves for researchers of prewar blues music.

I am indebted to Erik Anderson of the University of Minnesota Press for recruiting and encouraging me to write this book.

Finally, a very special thanks to my friends and family for their support and encouragement during the three decades that this book has been in progress: Jim Crockett, Ira Fried, Joe Gore, Steve Hilla, Don Menn, Tom Mulhern, Arthur Obrecht, John Obrecht, Tom and Kathy Obrecht, James Rotondi, Jon Sievert, George and Marie Staley, Rosedell Thomas, Sheridan and Betsey Warrick, and Tom Wheeler. Most of all, blessings on my wife and daughter, Michelle and Ava, for being my heart, soul, and inspiration.

Record companies during the 1920s marketed 78s by African Americans as "race records," sometimes featuring racist stereotypes in their advertisements. Courtesy Tim Gracyk.

Introduction

THE FIRST GREAT FLOWERING OF BLUES RECORDING began in the early 1920s with the rise of "classic" women singers such as Mamie Smith, Alberta Hunter, Ida Cox, Bessie Smith, and Ma Rainey. By the end of the decade, a dazzling array of male stars had made it onto record as well. This wonderfully fertile era, which laid the groundwork for virtually all the guitar-based blues music played today, came to an end with the onset of the Great Depression.

This book profiles the most prominent singer-guitarists who made influential and enduring recordings during the Roaring Twenties. Many other now-famous musicians were also performing guitar blues during this era—Big Bill Broonzy, Blind Boy Fuller, Blind Gary Davis, Memphis Minnie, Son House, and Lead Belly, to name a few—but the majority of their recordings came during the 1930s and afterward.

The first strains of blues music echoed across the American South, most likely around the beginning of the twentieth century. The exact origins of the blues are obscured in a swirling milieu of field hollers and work songs, African music, spirituals, ragtime, minstrel fare, folk tunes, parlor music, and other musical styles, but one fact is certain: since the mid-1920s, the blues and the guitar have traveled side by side.

In his 1941 autobiography, *Father of the Blues,* songwriter and bandleader W. C. Handy provided the earliest known description of a blues guitarist. Handy wrote of visiting the Mississippi Delta in 1903. One night while waiting for a train, he fell asleep in the Tutwiler station. A strange sound unlike any he had heard before suddenly awoke him. "A lean, loose-jointed Negro had commenced plunking a guitar beside me while I slept," Handy wrote. "His clothes were rags; his feet peeped out of his shoes. His face had on it some of the sadness of the ages. As he played, he pressed a knife on the strings of the guitar in a manner popularized by the Hawaiian guitarists who used steel bars. The effect was unforgettable. His song, too, struck me instantly: 'Goin' where the Southern cross the Dog.' The singer repeated the line three times, accompanying himself on the guitar with the weirdest music I had ever heard."[1] The unknown musician Handy observed was singing about Moorhead, Mississippi, where the Southern Railroad crossed the Yazoo-Delta Railroad, nicknamed "the Yellow Dog." Twenty years later, Sylvester Weaver, the first blues guitarist on record, would use the same slide technique while making his historic recording of "Guitar Rag."

Within a few years of W. C. Handy's sighting, blues had proliferated across the American South. According to early commentators, this music was most popular along the Mississippi River, where it was spread by riverboats and medicine shows and soon resounded in African American communities of all sizes. Perry Bradford, who in 1920 composed and oversaw the recording of the first blues record sung by an African American, wrote in his 1965 autobiography, *Born with the Blues,* that "the South was especially crazy about the blues, a cry of a broken heart that echoed from every levee and bayou up and down the Mississippi River."[2] All along, Bradford claimed, he was certain Southerners—black and white—would buy blues 78s: "They understand blues and jazz songs, for they've heard blind men on street corners in the South playing guitars and singing 'em for nickels and dimes ever since their childhood days."[3]

On the surface, the blues seemed simple enough. The songs, wrote W. C. Handy, "consisted of simple declarations expressed usually in three lines and set to a kind of earth-born music that was familiar throughout the Southland."[4] In the traditional twelve-bar blues Handy describes, two identical or similar vocal lines were typically answered by a third line. The whole verse was sung with suitable passion over a pattern involving three chords set to a straightforward or propulsive rhythm. There were many variations to this format, as heard in such classic eight-bar blues as "Key to the Highway," "Sitting on Top of the World," and "Trouble in Mind." When the spirit moved them, early blues guitarists such as Blind Lemon Jefferson and Lonnie Johnson would play elaborate solos that extended beyond a strict bar count, just as their disciples Lightnin' Hopkins, John Lee Hooker, and others would in the years after World War II.

Unlike the field hollers and work songs, the earliest blues songs were often music of leisure. Unlike ballads, they allowed the singer complete self-expression. A bluesman could brag, nag, howl at heaven, dis those he labored for, or seduce with passionate come-ons. He could fashion himself into a hero, victim, or savior. But despite their popularity, blues songs were not always accepted by members of the communities in which they were performed. To many, especially preachers and "churchified" folk, the blues was sometimes deemed "devil's music," fit only for field workers and totally unacceptable. As Johnny Shines, a bluesman who traveled with Robert Johnson in the 1930s, recalled, "When I was a kid, if a person heard you singing the blues and recognized your voice, you couldn't go down to their house, around their daughters."[5]

To some, even the guitar itself was taboo. When young W. C. Handy proudly brought one home, his father forced him to swap it for a dictionary. Even in high society, the blues had its detractors. Handy recounted how, in 1936, the eminent critic Deems Taylor introduced the Paul Whiteman Orchestra's performance of "St. Louis Blues" by quipping, "There are two schools of thought regarding the invention of the blues. One regards it as an event equal in importance to Edison's invention of the incandescent light. The other is inclined to classify it rather with Lincoln's assassination."[6]

Many first-generation bluesmen lived in a dangerous and unforgiving environment. This was especially true in the American South, where long hours of backbreaking labor, low pay, and the easily rigged sharecropping system kept plantation hands in virtual servitude. In the land of Jim Crow laws, even the slightest infraction (such as an African American male attempting to use a "white's only" drinking fountain, failing to step off the sidewalk to make way for a white woman, or gazing too long in the "wrong direction") could lead to torture and death by lynching. Against these impossible odds, bluesmen found shelter, relief, and an unsurpassed means for self-expression in their music. In the process, they created an enduring form of music that continues to enrich us all.

In the early days, blues songs were accompanied by acoustic instruments—just about every imaginable configuration of fiddle, piano, harmonica, banjo, washtub bass, horns, drums, washboard, and homemade instruments. In rural areas, singers most often accompanied themselves with an inexpensive acoustic guitar. "You couldn't fool with the pianos much," Son House explained to Jeff Todd Titon in *Living Blues,* "'cause they'd be too much to move all the time. Have to go and get a bunch—a team or mules and everything else to move it from place to place."[7] The banjo's staccato nature didn't lend itself to the vocal-sounding accompaniment preferred for blues or gospel, whereas the guitar, with its warmth and deep resonance, was perfectly suited, and its sustaining notes could be bent or bottlenecked. To expand their guitar's sonic palette, many blues guitarists learned to tune their strings into a chord, such as the open-D tuning (D, A, D, F#, A, D, going from the lowest string to the highest) favored by Blind Willie Johnson and Elmore James, and the banjo-derived open-G tuning (D, G, D, G, B, D) heard in the repertoires of Blind Willie McTell, Robert Johnson, Muddy Waters, and countless others.

African Americans had been performing blues music in various forms for about two decades before the recording of blues music for the African American audience commenced. As Jim O'Neal, founding editor of *Living Blues* magazine, points out, "The first recordings of blues were by white bands and singers, beginning in 1915, and these were not targeting the African American audience. Also, nearly everyone points to Mamie Smith as the first African American singer to record blues, but vaudevillian Bert Williams recorded three blues in 1919-20 before Mamie recorded 'Crazy Blues.' Williams's blues did not create a blues craze or lead to the 'race record' industry, however, whereas Mamie's did. Williams's records sold mostly to whites in the pre-race record era."[8]

Before 1920, record companies had assumed that African Americans couldn't—or wouldn't—buy record players or 78s. Then, in 1920, Mamie Smith's "Crazy Blues," the first recording of an African American woman singing the blues, revolutionized popular music. The release of "Crazy Blues" sparked a scramble among record company executives to record female blues singers. Witnesses claimed that after the release of "Crazy Blues," the song could be heard through the open windows of virtually any African American neighborhood in America. "That record turned around the recording industry," remembered New Orleans jazzman Danny Barker. "Every family had a phonograph in their house, specifically behind Mamie Smith's first record."[9]

The female singers that OKeh, Victor, Columbia, Black Swan, and other labels scouted and recorded during this heady era of classic blues, which lasted all of about three years, were not the downhome country singers who would record later in the 1920s. Rather they were primarily the glittering, glamorous, and savvy veterans of tent shows, minstrel troupes, and the vaudeville stage. These mavericks defied stereotypes, and there wasn't an Aunt Jemima among them (with the possible exception of Edith Wilson, who became the voice of Aunt Jemima on the radio). Their lyrics were often

erotic, frank, and cynical. Those who became most influential (Ma Rainey, Bessie Smith, and Ida Cox) had been performing blues for many years before their first recording sessions. Others emerged from black vaudeville and found quick fame and riches, only to be plunged back into obscurity and poverty. By the close of the 1920s, all the classic blueswomen would see their popularity eclipsed by male artists such as Blind Lemon Jefferson, Big Bill Broonzy, Lonnie Johnson, and Tampa Red—exceptional singer-guitarists all.

The success of Mamie Smith's first 78s inaugurated the 1920s blues boom. This advertisement appeared in the trade publication *The Talking Machine World* on April 15, 1921. Courtesy Tim Gracyk.

Those who knew him described Sylvester Weaver as dapper, considerate, and well loved. Courtesy Guido van Rijn.

OKeh

8109-B   Guitar Solo

GUITAR RAG
(Sara Martin-Sylvester Weaver)
SYLVESTER WEAVER

GENERAL PHONOGRAPH CORPORATION NEW YORK

The earliest known recording of a blues guitar instrumental, Sylvester Weaver's "Guitar Blues" was paired with "Guitar Rag" on OKeh 8109. The label credited the composition to Weaver and Sara Martin. Courtesy Roger Misiewicz and Helge Thygesen.

SYLVESTER WEAVER

The First Blues Guitarist on Record

OKEH RECORDS CALLED HIM "The Man with the Talking Guitar" and claimed "he certainly plays 'em strong on his big mean, blue guitar."[1] Sylvester Weaver found his place in history on October 24, 1923, when he fingerpicked simple, lonesome-sounding accompaniment to vaudeville singer Sara Martin's "Longing for Daddy Blues," and then picked up the tempo for the descending bass runs and more ambitious chords of her "I've Got to Go and Leave My Daddy Behind." In the process, Weaver became the first guitarist to back a blues singer on record. Nine days later, Weaver became the first guitarist to record a blues instrumental, waxing "Guitar Blues" and "Guitar Rag." The original 78 release, OKeh 8109, credited both Martin and Weaver as composers.

A slow, simple instrumental, "Guitar Blues" interspersed slide melodies with sparse, sliding chords. Weaver's rollicking "Guitar Rag" proved a far more significant recording. Playing with gusto in open-D tuning, Weaver conjured traces of ragtime and Hawaiian music in his memorable melodies. The song had wings. Weaver recut "Guitar Rag" in 1927 with stronger bass lines and a new middle section. This version influenced many white musicians and spawned an enduring Western swing hit, Bob Wills's 1936 "Steel Guitar Rag" featuring steel guitarist Leon McAuliffe. The song has been a country staple ever since. It also resonated through bluesmen, most notably Earl Hooker, one of Chicago's finest slide guitarists in the 1950s and 1960s.

When Weaver made his breakthrough 1923 recordings, capturing the sound of guitar and banjo solos proved challenging. Just a year or two before, Nick Lucas had played the first notable guitar instrumentals on record, "Pickin' the Strings" and "Teasin' the Frets." While neither of these recordings are blues songs, Nick's description of the session provides insight into the technology used to record the first wave of blues guitarists. Nick detailed:

> We always had trouble with the recording dates, because in those days they had the old cylinder wax. They had a big box in the back, and they kept all these waxes in the box always heated up. And the wax was pretty thick. We only had one horn to catch all the music into the cylinder to record. We didn't have microphones—this was the days before microphones. And we had the conventional combination, like three saxes and two trumpets and a trombone, piano, tuba, and a rhythm banjo. Guitar was unheard of. And we—that means the tuba and myself—had to sit *way* back in the studio, because when you blow notes out of a tuba, if it's too loud, that needle would jump off the cylinder and they'd have to start all over again. Very sensitive. And the banjo was the same thing, because it was a penetrating instrument. So I thought up an idea one morning of bringing my guitar to the studio. And [band leader] Sam Lanin says, "What you gonna do with that?" I said, "Well, Sam, I'm having so damn much trouble with the banjo, let me try the guitar." He said, "Well, Nick, they won't hear it." I said, "Well, put me closer to the horn." So he got me right under the horn.
>
> Now, this is a great, big horn. Visualize a great big horn, like you see advertised by the Victor Phonograph Company, the great big one with the dog. Well, that's what we had. So he put me under the horn, and the instrument was there. The rhythm was smoother, and we didn't have any trouble with the needle jumping out of the grooves. That was the beginning of me playing guitar on record dates. Now, I would say that was around 1921 or '22, something like that.[2]

Weaver was surely recorded the same way at his 1923 sessions, and it's likely he played lap-style.

Sylvester Weaver was born on July 25, 1896, in the Smoketown neighborhood of Louisville, Kentucky. His father, Walter Weaver, had migrated there from Mississippi during the 1880s.[3] Some parts of this historic neighborhood in Louisville's industrial section were little more than sooty tracks of tenements, but Smoketown was also home to many businesses owned by middle-class and professional African Americans. Weaver's first wife was Anna Myers, and he served briefly in the army during World War I. After 1918 he worked as a day laborer and made nightly rounds of Smoketown saloons and speakeasies, performing as a solo guitarist and with a jug band. He was active in the church throughout his life and, according to friends who knew him during the early 1920s, didn't see a conflict between playing blues music and being a churchgoer.

At the time of Weaver's first recording sessions, Sara Martin was already an established star, having released nearly two dozen 78s accompanied by top-flight accompanists such as Fats Waller, Clarence Williams, Sidney Bechet, and W. C. Handy's Orchestra. Apparently the first records featuring blues guitar sold well. An OKeh advertisement proclaimed: "Sara Martin discovered the clever idea of making recordings with a guitar accompaniment, and the first records of this kind put out have made remarkable impressions in all parts of the country. Sylvester Weaver plays his guitar in a highly original manner, which consists chiefly of sliding a knife up and down the strings while he picks with the other hand. His guitar solos, No. 8109, are having wide sales."[4] A delighted Ralph S. Peer of General Phonograph Corp. wrote a letter to Sara Martin informing her that "'Roamin' Blues' with guitar accompaniment is the biggest seller you have had since [1922's] 'Sugar Blues.' It might be well for you to rearrange your act so that this is your feature number using guitar accompaniment. It seems

Sylvester Weaver and singer Sara Martin recorded and toured together from 1923 through 1927. Courtesy Tim Bogert.

to me that this would make a wonderful encore number to be used very near the end of your act."[5]

Soon other classic women blues singers began featuring guitar accompaniment. By January 1924, Bessie Smith, Clara Smith, and Virginia Liston had recorded with guitarists—Weaver may, in fact, be the guitarist on Liston's "Jail House Blues."[6] Ida Cox and Ma Rainey followed suit a couple of months later. OKeh Records naturally paired Martin and Weaver for several follow-up sessions. In March 1924, the duo recorded three 78s in Atlanta. Weaver played rudimentary banjo on "Everybody's Got the Blues" and "My Man Blues," and easygoing guitar on "Pleading Blues," "Every Woman Needs a Man," "Got to Leave My Home Blues," and "Poor Me Blues." In May, Weaver backed Martin in New York City on "If I Don't Find My Brown I Won't Be Back at All." Around this time, Weaver recorded four more guitar instrumentals: "Weaver's Blues," "Smoketown Strut," "Mixing Them Up in 'C,'" and "I'm Busy and You Can't Come In." Played without a slide on a slightly out-of-tune guitar, these rudimentary, ragtime-influenced tunes provide early examples of string bending. A year later, Weaver and Martin were back in the studio, this time in St. Louis working alongside violinist E. L. Coleman and banjoist Charles Washington. In addition to accompanying Martin on several songs, Weaver played the muted slide guitar on Coleman's mournful "Steel String Blues."

Sylvester Weaver and Sara Martin went on tour together. British blues historian Paul Oliver writes that when Lonnie Johnson saw them in 1925, "Johnson was very impressed

Sylvester Weaver
Exclusive OKeh Artist
Wants you to hear one of his best OKeh Records:
8207—10 in.—75¢
Weaver's Blues
Mixing Them Up in "C"

Recorded in 1924, "Weaver's Blues" and "Mixing Them Up in 'C'" showcased early examples of string bending. OKeh Records listed the 78's price as seventy-five cents. Courtesy Guido van Rijn.

by Weaver's guitar playing—in fact he very seldom spoke about anyone else's work, but Weaver obviously (in person anyway) was someone he respected."[7] The similarities in their guitar approaches and "women are trouble"-themed lyrics suggest that Weaver exerted an influence on the younger Johnson.

Between sessions and theater appearances with Sara Martin, Weaver worked in Louisville's Smoketown section, where he lived at 727 Fenzer Street. For a while he labored as a packer for a clothing manufacturer. When he and his wife moved to an apartment house in a wealthier section of town, he became a janitor.[8] On occasion he worked as a talent scout. Helen Humes, who began recording in 1927, credited Weaver with discovering her in Louisville. "We were playing at a theater," she told Mike Joyce in *Cadence* magazine, "and this fellow Sylvester Weaver, he was one of the great guitar players and blues singers, he came down there and heard me and he got in touch with Mr. Rockwell [of OKeh Records] and had him come to Louisville to hear me."[9] On Weaver's recommendation, Humes was signed. "When I made my second session in New York," she wrote to producer Guido van Rijn in 1980, "my mother let me go with Mr. and Mrs. Weaver. He used to play the T.O.B.A. [black vaudeville] circuit and traveled the South. He was very well known down there. I've never heard no one say a bad thing about Mr. Weaver. All his Smoketown friends adored him. He was so nice + friendly and everybody in Ky. adored him."[10]

After a three-year hiatus, Weaver resurrected his recording career in April 1927. As part of Martin–Weaver–Withers, a trio with Sara Martin and her husband, Hayes B. Withers, he provided vocal and guitar accompaniment to the moving spiritual sides "Where Shall I Be?" and "I Am Happy in Jesus." He also backed Martin on the blues songs "Gonna Ramble Blues" and "Teasing Brown Blues," which came out credited to Sally Roberts. The label advertised "Teasing Brown Blues" as "the best 'scare' record OKeh has had in a long, long time." Weaver then recorded two of his own vocal-guitar blues, singing "True Love Blues" and "Poor Boy Blues" with a strong, world-weary voice. Once again, his guitar tuning sounds imprecise. Weaver next recut "Guitar Rag," delivering his finest guitar performance on record. On OKeh 8480, this new version was paired with his six-string banjo instrumental "Damfino Stump." At the same session he also cut the ragtimey "Six String Banjo Piece," a stronger performance than "Damfino Stump" that was withheld from release.[11]

In August 1927, Weaver participated in his final session with Sara Martin, playing slide on the mournfully slow "Loving Is What I Crave" and straight guitar accompaniment on the somnambulistic "On'ry Blues." They ended their studio partnership with the Sally Roberts-credited "Useless Blues" and "Black Hearse Blues." On his own, Weaver cut four new songs. The so-sad "Dad's Blues"—"I almost cursed the day that my baby boy was born"—came out backed with the equally down-hearted "What Makes a Man Blue":

> I'd rather be dead, laid in my lonesome
>   grave,
> I'd rather be dead, laid in my lonesome
>   grave,
> [Than] Have a monkey woman taking
>   me to be her slave.[12]

TEASING BROWN BLUES

Sally Roberts sings to a
guitar accompaniment
by
Sylvester Weaver
NO. 8485   10 in.—75c.
"TEASING BROWN BLUES"
"GONNA RAMBLE BLUES"

Teasing Brown Blues is the best "scare" record Okeh has had in a long, long time.

They'll be playing it in all the Okeh dealers' stores.

OKeh Records gave Sylvester Weaver top billing in an advertisement for Sally Roberts's "Teasing Brown Blues." The singer was actually Sara Martin. Courtesy Guido van Rijn.

He stayed on the theme of betrayal for "Can't Be Trusted Blues," issued paired with "Penitentiary Bound Blues":

> *Thought I was going to the workhouse, my heart was filled with strife,*
> *Thought I was going to the workhouse, my heart was filled with strife,*
> *But I'm going to the penitentiary, the judge sentenced me for life.*[13]

OKeh turned up the drama for their ad for this release, depicting a mournful minstrel-style convict wearing a ball and chain. The text read, "Low boomed moans, tired sad tones creep deeper and deeper in your heart and hold you to the spell of . . . Penitentiary Bound Blues."[14]

As the session neared its end, Weaver recorded two guitar duets with Walter Beasley, who was reportedly from Louisville. The beautiful but unreleased-at-the-time "Soft Steel Piston" featured Beasley playing rhythm beneath Weaver's jaunty slide melody. The duo reconvened in a New York studio in November 1927. They began on the twenty-sixth with "Chittlin Rag Blues," with Weaver sliding solos and singing with a strong voice:

> *They served you whiskey strong as nitroglycerine,*
> *They served you whiskey just as strong as nitroglycerine,*
> *And when you drink it, makes you feel so doggone mean.*[15]

As soon as they finished this, Weaver and Beasley backed Helen Humes on six songs. The standouts—"Cross-Eyed Blues" and "Garlic Blues"—featured Weaver playing adept slide while Beasley added bass lines and pluck-and-strum rhythms.

The next day, Weaver and Beasley kicked off the session with "Railroad Porter Blues," during which Weaver sang of passengers referring to a porter as "rastus"—a demeaning term even then. He ended the song with the verse:

> *Poor railroad porter, hates to leave his wife at home,*
> *Poor railroad porter, hates to leave his wife at home,*
> *'Cause she starts to cheating just as soon as he is gone.*[16]

The 78's flip side, the penitentiary-themed "Rock Pile Blues," moved to a slow, stately pace. Recorded at the same time, Weaver and Beasley's picturesque "Me and My Tapeworm"—"I'm a greedy glutton, eat fifty times a day"—was deemed unworthy of release. As the session progressed, Weaver and Beasley cut "Devil Blues" and "Polecat Blues," which has a superior twelve-bar slide section. Then Helen Humes was ushered into the studio for a trio of songs with two-guitar accompaniment: "Alligator Blues," "Nappy Headed Blues," and "Race Horse Blues." Weaver and Beasley finished the session with two guitar duets, the loose, good-time "Bottle Neck Blues," with its propulsive bass slides, and W. C. Handy's "St. Louis Blues." OKeh credited this 78 to "Weaver and Beasley."

On November 30, the duo recorded four Walter Beasley releases. Beasley, about whom little is known, was a rougher-sounding singer than Weaver but effective nonetheless. His version of "Georgia Skin" featured a line familiar to Cream fans: "When you lose your money, honey, don't lose your mind." "Southern Man Blues" borrowed from Blind Lemon Jefferson's "Match Box Blues," released earlier that year. Beasley's other 78 featured "Toad Frog Blues" and "Sore Feet Blues." Weaver made the most of his role as second guitarist, interspersing searing slide with nicely fingerpicked straight guitar. The duo concluded the day with Weaver's baby-you-gonna-die "Black Spider Blues."

OKeh's ad for "Black Spider Blues" showed a woman sprinting away from an oversized snake and spider, with the copy, "A Rattlesnake is dangerous, but a Black Spider is worser still."[17]

Why didn't Sylvester Weaver record again? "After 1927," explains Pen Bogert, who has extensively researched the Louisville scene, "Sylvester Weaver hardly played guitar at all." This detail helps explain why many blues researchers were stumped trying to find people in Smoketown who knew him as a musician. Around 1929, while still living in Smoketown, Weaver became a chauffeur and

Sylvester Weaver and Walter Beasley recorded "Bottle Neck Blues" and several other guitar duets in 1927. Courtesy Roger Misiewicz and Helge Thygesen.

butler for a wealthy Louisville family, a position he held for the rest of his life. He remarried in 1943. "Black and white," continues Pen, "people who knew Weaver said he was admired and respected in Smoketown. When asked to characterize him, they all used expressions like 'very good gentleman,' 'a neat dresser,' 'just a fine guy.' I get the impression he was a careful, somewhat conservative man, and this shows in his music."[18] Weaver was residing at 2001 Old Shepardville Road in Louisville when he fell victim to carcinoma of the tongue on April 4, 1960. Thirty-two years later, Bogert's KYANA Blues Society erected a headstone on his grave.

In 1976 blues researcher Paul Garon located Sylvester's second wife, Dorothy, who claimed she'd never heard him play. She pulled out Weaver's 78 collection and the music items from his old scrapbook. The records were no great shakes: four of Sylvester's own, three with Sara Martin, five or six other blues. The scrapbook, though, was another matter. Weaver saved telegrams, letters, ads, newspaper clippings, and royalty statements from publisher Clarence Williams. An assortment of these papers appears in *Living Blues,* no. 52.

According to the documents, Weaver's famous 78 of "Guitar Blues"/ "Guitar Rag" brought him less than fifty dollars in composer royalties, and Jim O'Neal speculated that about 5,438 copies of the disc were sold. "OKeh apparently paid Weaver $25 per side for 'recording work' on the songs he wrote and recorded," O'Neal detailed in *Living Blues.* "This sum may have been paid either as an advance on royalties or in addition to the less than one-half cent per side composer's royalties. While Weaver obviously never achieved riches through recording, it should be noted that he was paid substantially more in both recording fees and royalties than were many famous blues artists in the '30s and '40s, when payments of $5 to $15 per side and royalties of 15 percent of one cent per record were common."[19]

Among the scrapbook items was a tantalizing ad from the June 12, 1926, issue of *Chicago Defender,* an important Chicago-based African American newspaper that was carried coast-to-coast by railroad porters. The clipping announced a spectacular benefit for a musicians local, held at the Coliseum that evening. The "Cabaret and Style Show" starred Sara Martin, Clarence Williams, Shelton Brooks, Sylvester Weaver, Bertha "Chippie" Hill, Lonnie Johnson, Louis Armstrong, Butterbeans and Susie, and others. Besides a fashion show, giveaways, a Charleston contest, a radio broadcast, the "taking of moving pictures," and the "fifteen hottest dance orchestras," the ad promised that "famous race stars will show how OKeh race records are recorded." All for an admission of $1.10![20]

The first commercially successful male blues singer, Papa Charlie Jackson played a six-string Gibson GB, for "guitar-banjo." Courtesy of the author.

PAPA CHARLIE JACKSON

Six-String Stylist,
Flat-Picking Pioneer

THE FIRST COMMERCIALLY SUCCESSFUL male blues artist, Papa Charlie Jackson sang with a relaxed, confident voice and usually played an unusual six-string guitar-banjo. He began recording for Paramount in 1924 and produced nearly three dozen 78s by 1930. His versions of "Salty Dog," "Shake That Thing," "Alabama Bound," and "Spoonful" set the template for many covers to come. Playing finger-style or with a flat pick, Papa Charlie conjured a strong, staccato attack on his big guitar-banjo. His unstoppable rhythms were perfectly suited for dancing, and he was one of the first bluesmen to flat-pick solos on record.

Even during his prime, Papa Charlie's old-time approach must have seemed an anachronism. But like Jim Jackson, Gus Cannon, Charley Patton, Henry Thomas, Lead Belly, and other recording artists born in the 1880s or earlier, his non-blues records struck a resonant chord among listeners and provide us with examples of what African American music sounded like before the turn of the century. Jackson, most likely born in New Orleans on November 10, 1887, had a special affinity with ragtime and minstrel fare, and it is likely he toured with medicine and minstrel shows before World War I.

By 1920 Papa Charlie Jackson had settled in Chicago, where he gave guitar lessons, worked in clubs, and played for tips along

Charlie Jackson

FROM the ancient.—historical city of New Orleans, came Charlie Jackson —a witty—cheerful—kind hearted man —who, with his joyous sounding voice and his banjo, sang and strummed his way into the hearts of thousands of people. When he first contracted to sing and play for Paramount —many pessimistic persons laughed, and said they were certain no one wanted to hear comedy songs sung by a man strumming a banjo. But it wasn't long before they realized how wrong they were. Charlie and his records took the entire country by storm, and now—people like nothing better than to come home after a tiring and busy day and play his records. His hearty voice and gay, harmonious strumming on the banjo, causes their cares and worries to dwindle away, and gives them a careful frame of mind, and makes life one sweet song.

Papa Charlie Jackson's bio page in the 1927 promotional booklet *The Paramount Book of Blues*. Courtesy of the author.

Maxwell Street, probably performing ragtime. Reverend Thomas A. Dorsey, who recorded blues as Georgia Tom, explained to *Living Blues* that when he arrived in Chicago from Atlanta in 1919, "Wasn't much the blues then. Ragtime. See, you didn't have the blues singers. The blues wasn't recognized until the blues singers got a break, till they got a chance [to record], see. And then the blues began to spread. Blues singers came in by the score. Well, they had had them before, but they had no place to sing them, to exhibit what they had. And when they started to making these records, of blues singers, that was all we all needed."[1]

The Paramount Book of Blues, a strangely punctuated 1927 promotional booklet, gave this insight into Papa Charlie Jackson:

> From the ancient-historical city of New Orleans, came Charlie Jackson—a witty-cheerful-kind hearted man—who, with his joyous sounding voice and his banjo, sang and strummed his way into the hearts of thousands of people. When he first contracted to sing and play for Paramount—many pessimistic persons laughed, and said they were certain no one wanted to hear comedy songs sung by a man strumming a banjo. But it wasn't long before they realized how wrong they were. Charlie and his records took the entire country by storm, and now—people like nothing better than to come home after a tiring and busy day and play his records. His hearty voice and gay, harmonious strumming on the banjo, causes their cares and worries to dwindle away, and gives them a careful frame of mind, and makes life one sweet song.[2]

Decked in a fashionable three-piece suit, Papa Charlie stared calmly into the lens for the promotional photograph that accompanied the write-up. An inscrutable, serious-looking man with a dimpled chin and long, tapering fingers, he held his guitar-banjo. Norman Blake, renowned bluegrass flat-picker, describes the instrument:

> Papa Charlie's holding a Gibson GB, for "guitar-banjo," and I have one from 1921. This particular model is a very primitive open-back with a huge fourteen-inch head—I call mine "Goliath." It has a regular

old-style Gibson laminated guitar neck with sort of a moccasin-type headstock rather than the snake-head variety. The three-on-a-plate tuners are like those on the old Gibson guitars, and it also has a short trapeze-type tailpiece and a white ivoroid pickguard that mounts and slides on a rod. The instrument is soft-sounding compared to what you generally think of as being in the banjo family. This is probably because the sound is spread out by that big head. When Papa Charlie just strums rhythm chords on some things, he gets kind of a funky, sloshy sound, and I like his general looseness.[3]

Despite labels and ads listing him as playing ukulele or "blues banjo," he usually recorded with his guitar-banjo or a standard acoustic guitar.

The Paramount Book of Blues also included sheet music with vocal and piano music and often inaccurate lyric transcriptions for a few of his songs. "Shake That Thing," "Salty Dog," and "Alabama Bound" listed Charlie Jackson as the songwriter, while on "Up the Way Bound" he shared credit with singer Lillian Brown.

Most of Jackson's sessions were held in Chicago. He made his first recordings, "Papa's Lawdy Lawdy Blues" and "Airy Man Blues," in mid- to late August 1924. His guitar-banjo set in standard A=440 guitar tuning, he played his debut selection in the key of E. But despite its title, winsome humming, and plaintive refrains of "Lordy Lord, Lordy Lord, Lawd, Lawd, Lawd," the first tune is more of an eight-bar vaudeville number than a traditional blues. Fast, danceable, and expertly fingerpicked, "Airy Man Blues" mixed eight- and twelve-bar structures and is a direct precursor of Taj Mahal's "Fishin' Blues." The song's lyrics, which mention Chicago's State Street, suggest that the record's correct title should probably have been "Hairy Man Blues."

Paramount announced the release with an ad in the *Chicago Defender*. "Well Sir!" read the copy, "Here He Is at Last! Papa Charlie Jackson—the famous Blues-singing-Guitar-playing Man." Promoting Papa Charlie's "Original Lawdy, Lawdy Blues," the ad went on to

Paramount Records' debut Papa Charlie Jackson advertisement billed him as the "only man living who sings, self-accompanied, for Blues records." Months earlier, Atlanta's Ed Andrews had recorded a self-accompanied blues 78. Courtesy Alex van der Tuuk.

proclaim Jackson the "only man living who sings, self-accompanied, for Blues records."[4] This assertion was incorrect, though. Five months earlier, an OKeh field unit in Atlanta had recorded Ed Andrews, a rough-hewn country bluesman who accompanied himself on guitar. Two months after that, Johnny Watson had recorded as Daddy Stovepipe, accompanying himself on a guitar and harmonica, and Samuel Jones, a self-styled one-man band who called himself Stovepipe No. 1, had already played his first session.[5] The first Papa Charlie Jackson ad also assured readers "that this man Charlie can sing and play the Blues even better than a woman can." Meanwhile, the fine print listed titles by Trixie Smith, Ida Cox, Anna Lee Chisholm, and Ma Rainey.

Warm and humorous, Papa Charlie's follow-up release, the ragtimey, eight-bar "Salty Dog Blues," made him a recording star. The song conveyed the sly perspective of an "outside man":

> *Now, the scaredest I ever been in my life,*
> *Uncle Bud like to caught me kissin' his wife,*
> *Salty dog, you salty dog.*[6]

As the recording progressed, Jackson's chugging banjo rhythm sped up, perhaps the result of natural excitement or an engineer's nod that time was running out. On its flip side, "Salt Lake City Blues," Papa Charlie capped his first recording of a standard twelve-bar blues with a sure-handed solo.

Old-time New Orleans musicians recalled hearing filthier versions of "Salty Dog Blues" long before Papa Charlie's recording. And more versions followed. In May 1926 Clara Smith recorded an inoffensive version for Columbia. Two months later, Papa Charlie Jackson made an outstanding band version with Freddie Keppard's Jazz Cardinals featuring Johnny Dodds on clarinet. The session may have been a reunion of sorts, since Keppard, Dodds, and Jackson all hailed from New Orleans. The performance concluded with a rousing aside of "Papa Charlie done sung that song!" Originally released as Paramount 12399, the Keppard version of "Salty Dog" was reissued by other labels during the ensuing years, including a version on American Music and an interesting 1941 pressing issued by the United Hot Club of America.[7]

White country musicians picked up on Jackson's songs as well. In 1927, Opry star Kirk McGee did close covers of "Salty Dog Blues" and "Salt Lake City Blues" on Vocalion. "It was natural that Sam and Kirk McGee, who used to play with Uncle Dave Macon back in the old days, were borrowing some of Papa Charlie's stuff," says Norman Blake. "Because Papa Charlie flat-picked, he crossed the line towards hillbilly or country. He recorded during that good era when there wasn't exactly a distinction between black and white music and the musicians all kind of sounded the same when they played the mandolin, banjos, and fiddles."[8]

Jackson's unusual guitar-banjo sound brought him session work backing other blues artists. It's believed he accompanied warm and soulful Lottie Beaman on the October 1924 Paramount session for "Mama Can't Lose," with Jimmy Blythe on piano. This performance came out on Paramount credited to Lottie's real name, and on Silvertone credited to "Jennie Brooks." During April 1925 Jackson joined Ida Cox, one of the great classic blues singers, on the two-part "Mister Man," playing guitar-banjo and adding vocals. He rejoined Miss Cox in September for "How Long Daddy, How Long," playing sparse, quickly damped accompaniment to her elegant voice.

At the first of his own 1925 sessions, in January, Jackson reworked his "Lawdy, Lawd" motif in "The Cat's Got the Measles," a Murphy-Smiley composition that gathered traditional verses. He injected a fine low-register guitar-banjo solo into the suggestive "I Got What It Takes but It Breaks My Heart to Give It Away." Jackson's follow-up session that same month produced a memorable cover of the eight-bar "Shave 'Em Dry," which had already been recorded by Ma Rainey.

Its flip side, his original "Coffee Pot Blues," was set to the familiar "Sliding Delta" melody. While not nearly as salaciously funny as the novelty version recorded a decade later by Lucille Bogan, Jackson's "Shave 'Em Dry" did hint of the risqué:

> *Now just one thing, can't understand,*
> *Why a bow-legged woman likes a knock-kneed man,*
> *Mama can I holler, Daddy won't you shave 'em dry.*[9]

Papa Charlie Jackson struck pay dirt in May 1925 with his biggest hit record, "Shake That Thing." Decades later, Thomas A. Dorsey credited the 78 with inaugurating the 1920s hokum craze. After a novel stop-time solo, Jackson sang:

> *Now Grandpa Johnson grabbed sister Kate*
> *He shook her just like you shake the jelly from a plate,*
> *You gonna shake that thing,*
> *Aw, shake that thing,*
> *I'm getting sick and tired of telling you to shake that thing.*[10]

The success of Jackson's "Salty Dog Blues" and "Shake That Thing" reportedly convinced producer J. Mayo "Ink" Williams to scout and record Blind Blake and Blind Lemon Jefferson, who'd most likely been scouted by Art Laibly after being advised by Sam Price.[11] By year's end, "Shake That Thing" had been covered by Eva Taylor for OKeh and by Ethel Waters for Columbia. Within months, there were new versions out by Viola McCoy on Vocalion and by Jackson's label mates Viola Bartlette and Jimmie O'Bryant's Famous Original Washboard Band.

Jackson kept churning out records, usually producing one complete 78 per session. Around late May 1925 he and a talented unknown second banjoist recorded his sprightly "I'm Alabama Bound"—melodically similar to Charley Patton's later recording of "Elder Greene Blues"—and a nicely fingerpicked original called "Drop That

Sack." His sound was better captured at the July session for "Hot Papa Blues" and "Take Me Back Blues," with its memorable low-string solo presaging the guitar work on Blind Lemon Jefferson's 78s. The next month, Jackson took a noteworthy chord solo in the pimp tale "Mama Don't Allow It (And She Ain't Gonna Have It Here)."

In September 1925 Jackson made the first known recording of "Spoonful," titled "All I Want Is a Spoonful." The song was reputed to be sexually graphic—scandalously so—in its folk form, so Papa Charlie's version was considerably cleansed:

> *I told you once, this makes twice,*
> *That's the last time—don't you burn that rice,*
> *Because all I want, honey babe, is just a spoonful, spoonful.*
>
> *You can brown your gravy, fry your steak,*
> *Sweet mama don't make no mistake,*
> *'Cause all I want, honey babe, is just a spoonful, spoonful.*[12]

Its release was backed with the picturesque "Maxwell Street Blues," in which a man pleads for the release of his trick-turning gal.

Around November 21, 1925, Jackson trudged across Chicago's bleak winter landscape to record his wistful "I'm Going Where the Chilly Winds Don't Blow," followed by two takes of "Texas Blues"—one played on banjo, the other on an acoustic guitar. He demonstrated considerable finesse on the guitar version, playing dexterous chord voicings on the treble strings. His easy-rolling fingerpicking was reminiscent of Blind Blake's style, while one of the verses resurfaced a few years later in Blind Willie McTell's masterful "Travelin' Blues." Jackson produced two more 78s in January 1926, including "Let's Get Along" and an original guitar boogie, "Jackson's Blues."

Over the next year and a half, Jackson recorded only eight songs. His smooth, string-bending guitar performance on "Up the Way Bound" was similar to Robert Wilkins's style and perhaps gives

According to Paramount Records' 1925 ad, "'All I Want Is a Spoonful' combines snappy words, nifty tune, and some great guitar strumming by 'Papa.'" Courtesy Alex van der Tuuk.

credence to the rumor that Papa Charlie may have spent time living in Memphis. He also cut a banjo version of the tune. An unidentified second banjoist with a fabulous tremolo joined him at the March 1927 session for his original compositions "She Belongs to Me Blues" / "Coal Man Blues," reportedly the first electrically recorded Papa Charlie Jackson 78. An advertisement in the *Chicago Defender* credited the artists on "Coal Man Blues" as "Jackson and Jackson—two Banjos."[13]

Jackson's next studio date, in June 1927, teamed him with Lucille Bogan for "War Time Man Blues" and "Jim Tampa Blues." The sides capture a warm rapport, with Papa Charlie making asides and turning in a crackerjack performance on his guitar-banjo. During the instrumental section of his "War Time Man Blues," Lucille encouraged him with "Oh, play it, Papa Charlie, play it! Whoop that thing!" He laced "Jim Tampa Blues" with flat-picked chords, strong bass lines, and a fiery double-time break. During the same session, Papa Charlie played solo on "Skoodle Um Skoo," a lighthearted dance tune in the vein of "Shake That Thing" and some of the songs in Blind Blake's repertoire. Paired with another original, "Sheik of Desplaines Street," the 78 sold well, with "Skoodle Um Skoo" inspiring covers by Big Bill Broonzy and Seth Richard, who played twelve-string and kazoo on his version. Charlie himself recut the song in 1934.

By the end of 1927 Jackson had recorded three more titles under his own name. His original composition "Look Out Papa Don't Tear Your Pants" was a curious mix of Hawaiian music, ragtime syncopation, and risqué blues, all wrapped up in a bravura flat-picking performance. Jackson delivered the pimp imagery of its flip side, the rollicking foot-stomper "Baby Don't You Be So Mean," with falsetto flourishes. Around October 1927, he played guitar on the pop tune "Bright Eyes." The influence of Blind Lemon Jefferson's guitar approach resonates in the session's other side, "Blue Monday Morning Blues."

During January 1928, Papa Charlie Jackson delivered strong vocal performances on "I'm Looking for a Woman Who Knows How to Treat Me Right," backed with a countrified reading of "Long Gone Lost John." During "Long Gone Lost John" Jackson sings, "Now if anybody should ask you who composed this song, tell 'em Papa Charlie Jackson, then idle on." But the song had already been published in 1920 as "Long Gone John (From Bowling Green)" by W. C. Handy and lyricist Chris Smith. It was probably based on an old Kentucky folk song about an African American jail trusty who was set free to test the efficiency of a pack of bloodhounds. In Jackson's version, Long John fashions a pair of shoes with heels on both ends and makes it to town, where he visits his "brown" and knocks down a policeman before making a clean getaway to the Gulf of Mexico. On the Paramount release, the 78 was credited to Papa Charlie Jackson. On the less-expensive Broadway label, the artist was listed as "Charlie Carter." The 78 was reissued as a dub in England and Austria.

Jackson focused on hokum shtick on his next releases. The seductive "Ash Tray Blues" was backed with "No Need of Knockin' on the Blind," which details the Boccaccio-like goings-on in the marriage of an eighty-two-year-old man to a woman sixty years his junior. "I Like to Love My Baby" emphasized Jackson's rhythmic prowess and good-time scat singing, while "Baby—Papa Needs His Lovin'" recycled tried-and-true motifs.

Backed by "Good Doing Papa Blues," his "Lexington Kentucky Blues" was advertised in the *Chicago Defender,* December 1928, with a drawing of Jackson on a sideshow stage playing banjo for a hoochy-koochy dancer. "'Papa Charlie' Jackson went down to the great Kentucky State Fair last summer," claimed Paramount's copy, "and he must have had a wonderful time. All kinds of experiences, and he sings about what he did and what he saw in this 'Lexington Kentucky Blues,' as he plays a mean banjo accompaniment."[14]

Hard times for the blues: the whimsical "Ma and Pa Poorhouse Blues" told how Ma Rainey's bus got stolen and Papa Charlie had to pawn his big guitar-banjo. Courtesy Roger Misiewicz and Helge Thygesen.

During October 1928, Jackson joined Ma Rainey on a pair of minstrel-style duets. Derived from Victoria Spivey's popular "T.B. Blues," "Ma and Pa Poorhouse Blues" began with an exchange in which listeners hear how Papa Charlie had to pawn his big guitar-banjo and somebody stole Ma's bus. Learning they are both broke, the singers decide to go to the poorhouse together. Their next song,

"Big Feeling Blues," was destined to be Ma Rainey's final recording. Ma played a man-hungry woman to Papa Charlie's interested "big-kid man." Soon after this session, Paramount canceled Ma's contract. A Paramount executive reported to Charles Edward Smith during the 1950s that "Ma's down-home material had gone out of fashion."[15]

An all-star cast appeared on the two-part "Hometown Skiffle" 78. In this rare advertisement, Paramount Records changed the spelling of the title and misidentified photographs of Blind Blake and Blind Lemon Jefferson. Courtesy Robert Coon. Touchup by Susan Archie.

For a while Paramount continued to support Papa Charlie's 78s with catchy ads. The copy for "Jungle Man Blues," recorded on December 28, 1928, read like the script of a two-reel cliff-hanger: "As he sings this 'Jungle Man Blues,' he grabs the wild cat by the collar, looks the panther right in the eye, and asks the tiger what he has to say. Look at him—a rattle snake watch chain and a scorpion for a fob! 'Papa Charlie' Jackson, aided by his trusty banjo, sings this wild one on Paramount 12721."[16]

By late March 1929 Jackson had provided the voice of Dentist Jackson on Hattie McDaniel's two-part "Dentist Chair Blues." This blues singer would later win the 1939 Academy Award for Best Supporting Actress for her portrayal of Mammy in *Gone with the Wind*. On his ensuing recordings, Papa Charlie recycled previous material. For the lazy "Hot Papa Blues No. 2," he replaced the original version's flashy guitar-banjo runs with stock guitar accompaniment. He recast "Take Me Back Blues No. 2" as a slow-paced guitar blues. Paramount's ad for "Hot Papa Blues No. 2" was far more enthusiastic than the performance, depicting a dapper Papa Charlie strutting in front of a gang of flappers being held back by a police officer. "No wonder they all fall for him!" explained the copy. "He's just a red-hot papa in a class all by himself, and it takes a cop or two to hold the mamas back when he struts down the avenue. 'Papa Charlie' Jackson sure knows how to sing and play this kind of blues."[17] He also played guitar on the hokumy "We Can't Buy It No More."

That fall Jackson recorded "'Taint What You Got but How You Do It" / "Forgotten Blues," possibly in a temporary studio that had been set up in Milwaukee.[18] In late January 1930 he returned to Grafton to record "Papa Do Do Do Blues" / "I'll Be Gone Babe." He then yucked it up with his label mate on the two-part "Papa Charlie and Blind Blake Talk about It." Their guitar-banjo and guitar blended together nicely, and the emphasis was clearly on having a good time. The musicians exchanged good-natured banter, scat sang together, and stepped out on their instruments, with Jackson playing a memorable muted solo over Blake's accomplished big-band-style comping. Today this is considered one of Papa Charlie's rarest Paramount 78s, with only about a half dozen known copies in the possession of collectors.

In another cross-promotional effort, Paramount featured a segment of Papa Charlie's "Shake That Thing" on its two-part Paramount All Stars 78 of "Hometown Skiffle," advertised in February 1930 as a "descriptive novelty featuring Blind Lemon Jefferson, Blind Blake, Will Ezell, Charlie Spand, the Hokum Boys, Papa Charlie Jackson."[19] Papa Charlie would supply only one additional release for the label that had made him famous, the lackluster "You Got That Wrong" / "Self Experience," recorded on guitar in the first week of June 1930.

Jackson's next studio appearance, in June 1934, was as a sideman on Big Bill Broonzy's "At the Break of Day" / "I Want to Go Home," issued on Bluebird. Afterward, he reportedly backed Big Boy Edwards and Amos "Bumble Bee Slim" Easton on sessions. Jackson recorded his final pair of issued 78s in November 1934. Upbeat and very well-recorded, his new cover of "Skoodle Um Skoo," with its effective by-the-bridge banjo strums, was paired with the trucking "What's That Thing She's Shaking?" The less fancy "If I Got What You Want" / "You Put It In, I'll Take It Out" (actually a song about money) came out on OKeh and Vocalion. "Towards the end of his career," Samuel B. Charters described in *The Country Blues,* "he was used to cover hits by other singers. He was a tall, awkward man, unable to read or write. To record a new song he had to have someone sitting behind him whispering the words into his ear, just as many of the blind singers did."[20] Alex van der Tuuk points out that this information contradicts Jackson's 1920 census listing, which states that he was able to read and write, adding, "Mayo Williams, in a 1961 letter to Tony Standish, wrote that Jackson was an unlearned Creole."[21] Big Bill Broonzy, who claimed to have studied guitar with Jackson in the early 1920s, sat alongside him on March 8, 1935, when he made his final three records for ARC, which never issued them. Papa Charlie Jackson died in Chicago on May 7, 1938.

Cordially Yours Blind Lemon Jeffers

BLIND LEMON JEFFERSON

Popular from Coast to Coast

BLIND LEMON JEFFERSON, who began recording for Paramount Records circa late 1925, became the most famous bluesman of the Roaring Twenties. His 78s shattered racial barriers, becoming popular from coast to coast and influencing a generation of musicians. His best songs forged original, imagistic themes with inventive arrangements and brilliantly improvised solos. His lyrics create a unique body of poetry—humorous and harrowing, jivey and risqué, a stunning view of society from the perspective of someone near the bottom. To this day, he ranks among the most gifted and individualistic artists in blues history.

Jefferson was a serious showman, balancing a driving, unpredictable guitar style with a booming, two-octave voice. "He hollered like someone was hitting him all the time" is how Reverend Gary Davis described it.[1] Piercing enough to be heard above the clang and din of city streets, Jefferson's wailing vocals set him apart from his contemporaries. His guitar became a second voice that complemented

Paramount Records publicity photograph of Blind Lemon Jefferson, circa 1927. Courtesy of the author.

rather than repeated the melodies he sang. He often halted rhythm at the end of vocal lines to launch into elaborate solo flourishes. He could play in unusual meters with a great deal of drive and flash, and he was adept in many keys.

"His guitar never dominated his songs," says John Hammond. "It was so succinct. It was just perfect playing. He had a distinctive way of doing solos, and his voice was incredible! He could moan and howl and really put a song across. Blind Lemon influenced everybody, because his records in the twenties were all over the United States. He especially had an impact on a lot of white players—vocally more than with his guitar style. His guitar style was so advanced, unique, amazing, and just hard to do. Jimmie Rodgers in particular must have just flipped out over Lemon."[2]

Blind Lemon Jefferson became B.B. King's hero: "His way of execution left you with the *feeling* that you could hear someone else backing him up. And he had a special way of phrasing, too, that I don't hear from many people today. Anyone can play 64 notes in a bar, but to place just one or two in that same bar in just the right place, or maybe even let one go by, then double up on it in the next bar—that's something special. Blind Lemon was my idol."[3]

The first major publicity item about Blind Lemon Jefferson appeared in *The Paramount Book of Blues*:

Can anyone imagine a fate more horrible than to find that one is blind? To realize that the beautiful things one hears about—one will never see? Such was the heart-rending fate of Lemon Jefferson, who was born blind and realized, as a small child, that life had withheld one glorious joy from him—sight. Then—environment began to play its important part in his destiny. He could hear—and he heard the sad hearted, weary people of his homeland, Dallas—singing weird, sad melodies at their work and play, and unconsciously he began to imitate them— lamenting his fate in song. He learned to play a guitar, and for years he entertained his friends freely—moaning his weird songs as a means of forgetting his affliction. Some friends who saw great possibilities in

ꟷBlind Lemon Jefferson

AN anyone imagine a fate more horrible than to find that one is blind? To realize that the beautiful things one hears about — one will never see? Such was the heart-rending fate of Lemon Jefferson, who was born blind and realized, as a small child, that life had withheld one glorious joy from him — sight. Then — environment began to play its important part in his destiny. He could hear—and he heard the sad hearted, weary people of his homeland, Dallas — singing weird, sad melodies at their work and play, and unconsciously he began to imitate them — lamenting his fate in song. He learned to play a guitar, and for years he entertained his friends freely — moaning his weird songs as a means of forgetting his affliction. Some friends who saw great possibilities in him, suggested that he commercialize his talent — and as a result of following their advice — he is now heard exclusively on Paramount.

Blind Lemon Jefferson's bio page in *The Paramount Book of Blues.* Courtesy of the author.

him, suggested that he commercialize his talent—and as a result of following their advice—he is now heard exclusively on Paramount.[4]

Probably generated by a publicist who may have never met Jefferson, it's likely that little of this holds true. On to the facts.

The earliest known record of Blind Lemon Jefferson's life appears
in the 1900 U.S. Census records for Freestone County, Texas. The
original document for "Precinct 5, South End of Big Tehuacana
Creek" lists the names of eight members in the Jefferson family.
Each of their entries identifies them as "B," for black. Alex Jefferson is listed as "Head" of the household, and "farmer" is given as
his profession. His wife's name, less legibly scrawled, appears to be
"Clarricy." Since both of Blind Lemon's parents were born in Texas
before the end of the Civil War (his father in 1862 and his mother
two years earlier), it is possible they were born into slavery. In 1900
they had been married four years. The next members of the household are three children who share the last name of Banks: Alex's
stepdaughter Francis, born 1886, and stepsons Iricia, 1887, and
Clarrience, 1888. All of these children have "farm labor" listed as
their occupation. The last name for the next entry, Johnnie, born
1892, was originally written as "Jefferson," but this appears to have
been intentionally smudged, and he too is listed as a stepson. So
at least three of these children, and perhaps all four, are Clarricy's
children by another man, making them Blind Lemon's half siblings.
The remaining two household members share the last name of Jefferson: son Lemmon, as his name is spelled, and daughter Martha,
born 1896. Next to the name Lemmon is "Bl," most likely shorthand
for "blind." Lemmon's entry is the only one in his family to list a full
date of birth: "Sept. 4, 1893."[5]

The Jefferson family reappears in the 1910 census for Navarro
County, Precinct 6, Texas. Here Blind Lemon's parents are listed
as Alek, a forty-year-old farm laborer, and his wife Clarisa, a forty-
two-year-old laundress. A notation indicates that the pair had been

married twenty years. The entry for their son Lemmon shows he's sixteen and blind. Written into the space for describing his occupation is "None." Next come Lemmon's sisters: Martha, fourteen, a farm laborer; Mary, nine; Sibe, eight; and Gussie M., five. The census record also shows that they share their residence with a twenty-five-year-old farm laborer whose name appears to be Francis Quistan, and her ten-month-old granddaughter Annie.[6]

During the 1950s, author and record producer Samuel B. Charters drove an hour south of Dallas to the "rolling farmland" of Blind Lemon Jefferson's childhood. "From a small hill near Alec Jefferson's farmhouse in Couchman," Charters wrote, "you can see across the fields to the buildings of Mexia, Texas, twelve miles to the southwest. The scattered buildings of Wortham, Texas, stretch along the railroad tracks five or six miles to the west. There are fields of old oil rigs between the two towns. . . . The ground is black with oil waste, but the only signs of oil money in Wortham are three or four ugly church buildings, built out of brick and designed to resemble funeral parlors."[7]

As a child, Jefferson sang at the Shiloh Baptist Church in nearby Kirvin. Residents remembered him running with the other children through the fields and playing in the brush along Cedar Creek. "He'd run after them," Charters described, "stand listening to them cross the footlogs over the stream, then slowly walk the footlogs after them. The neighbors thought he had a kind of gift."[8] Some went so far as to say he was a magical child gifted with supernatural abilities. Around 1907, Charters reported, Lemon's brother Johnnie was crushed to death beneath a slow-moving freight train, which would account for the absence of his name in the 1910 census records.

By his teens Lemon had acquired a guitar, taught himself to play, and was performing under overhanging eaves of buildings in Wortham and Kirvin. Steve James, an expert purveyor of "archaic finger-style guitar," has extensively researched Jefferson's history.

James describes a conversation he had with retired Wortham postmaster Uel L. Davis Jr.

> Uel Davis remembered Lemon from before World War I, when his family owned a bank and pharmacy in downtown Wortham. When Uel was a little kid, it was a big treat for him and his friends to go downtown to see him. Lemon would come into town every Saturday when he was around and play in front of the bank from lunch time, when people were doing business in town, until dinner. He remembers Lemon having a tin cup stapled to the headstock of his guitar. Uel Davis was one of many informants who spoke about Lemon's uncanny ability to know what was going on, even though he had little or no sight at all. If you laughed at some line in his song, he'd put the cup right under your nose. I asked Uel about Lemon's lead boys, and he said that most of the time Lemon came to town by himself. He'd cross fences and walk down creek beds all by himself, using a walking stick. Uel also said that if he came with anybody, it would often be a mandolinist. Besides blues, they would play a variety of songs.[9]

While he was unable to find anyone who recalled music in Couchman before World War I, James has ideas about Jefferson's influences:

> Lemon was really steeped in the string band tradition. Although he recorded almost exclusively blues, I've heard accounts of him playing "The Chicken Reel" with a mandolin player, and all kinds of stuff. Lemon played mandolin, too. Blues was actually just part of the tremendous repertoire of the string band musicians, who also played ragtime. I imagine there were probably horn players in the area, too. There were also a lot of guys playing the piano, following the Santa Fe Railroad and going up and down the Brazos Bottom. And that's what Lemon essentially was—a man from the Brazos River Bottom. And these guys had a piano style that's very much Texas. The piano players Robert Shaw and Alex Moore were the tip of that iceberg that survived into the modern age. As you listen to them, you'll hear that they extend the bar structure of a song whenever they want to. If they've got another lick they want to play before they go to the IV, they do it. That was characteristic of the Santa Fe style in the first decade of the

century. Lemon played piano pretty competently, so I guess he must have been influenced by that too. Most of the guys who were really whipping it on guitar, playing anything more than a very linear style, were very pianistic, like Blind Blake. They played denser harmonies.[10]

Jefferson's venues soon included country suppers and parties at farms scattered around Couchman, Mexia, and as far north as Waxahachie. Like Mississippi juke joints, these were often rugged affairs, with freely flowing bootleg liquor and men hustling women. "They didn't do any proper kind of dancing, just stompin'," Blind Lemon's cousin Alec Jefferson told Charters. "He'd start singing about eight and go on until four in the morning. Sometime he'd have another fellow with him, playing a mandolin or a guitar and singing along, but mostly it would be just him, sitting there and playing and singing all night."[11]

Around 1912, Lemon Jefferson moved to Dallas. His next entry in the public record occurred on June 5, 1917, when he registered for the draft at Precinct 11 in Dallas. The original, handwritten copy of his registration card is on file in the National Archives. The document's first side lists his given name as Lemon Jefferson, his address as 1803 Preston, and his date of birth as October 15, 1894. Wortham, Texas, is his place of birth. His answer for line 7, "What is your present trade, occupation, or office?," is the word "No." By whom employed? "Nobody." Where employed? "Nowhere." Race? "Nigra." Jefferson gave his marital status as "Single," and he claimed an exemption from the draft on the grounds of being blind. The other side of the card describes Jefferson as being of "medium" height, "medium" build, and having black hair. The final annotation states, "Blind both eyes. Born blind." After Jefferson signed the document with an "X," the person who'd filled in the card for him wrote his first name on one side of his mark and his last name on the other.[12]

In his *Living Blues* article "Draft Card Blues," Jonathan Black pointed out, "The 1917 draft card is the only known document relating to Jefferson that we can be confident was created in the musician's presence. It is a legal document to which Jefferson himself attested."[13] An astute researcher, Black investigated the 1803 Preston address:

> A 1920 map prepared by the Sanborn Company shows 1803 Preston as a single-story wooden house less than 20 feet wide and 30 feet long. The structure was little more than a shotgun shack, lacking even the covered front porch common to most houses in the area. Immediately across Preston were the tracks of the Central Railroad, raised on an artificial mound of earth. Noise from the busy railroad would have been an almost constant factor in the lives of those living on Preston. But the house was conveniently located for Jefferson. It was less than a mile south of Deep Ellum, the center of commerce and nightlife for African-American Dallas during the teens and twenties. It was also the area most frequented by Jefferson and other blues musicians in Dallas, offering them the largest audiences and richest pickings.[14]

Today, Black notes, Jefferson's former residence "is long gone. The site itself is now occupied by an abandoned and decaying Bluebell creamery."[15]

During his years in Dallas, Blind Lemon Jefferson spent most of his time in Deep Ellum, the area near where Central Avenue crossed Elm Street. The neighborhood had dance halls, pawnshops, secondhand clothing stores, shoeshine parlors, and beer joints. Steve James retraced Lemon's old haunts:

> Deep Ellum—southern Elm Street—was the hangout. There was a train stop on Central where black laborers from the country would get off to go to Elm Street and raise hell. Right now that's where Highway 30 crosses Elm Street. Several blocks down from Elm, where Hall crosses Central, there was also a big black community called Freedmen's Town, which was established after the Civil War. Many blacks from the country moved there to work with the railroad and associated industries after a tremendous boll weevil blight took out the cotton industry around the turn of the century. People would walk from Freedmen's Town to Deep Ellum. There were several happening clubs

Jefferson's "Black Snake Moan No. 2" began with the announcement "Well, folks, Lemon is yet lookin' for his black snake mama." This print advertisement declares the record a hit. Courtesy Alex van der Tuuk.

where blues singers played on Elm Street in the twenties. There was the Green Parrot, the Tip Top, the Big Four. Ella B. Moore's Park Theater was another colored establishment.

Lemon used to walk up the central tracks with his stick and his guitar, and he'd play outside a theater, bank, or establishment where a lot of people were going to congregate. He'd play for tips all day, and then he'd pick up and go to a bar or a whorehouse at night. He lived somewhere along the central tracks in south Dallas. He probably moved around a bit, because he was also a bootlegger. I've also heard stories of him being a professional wrestler. I don't know how much credence to lend to that, but Deep Ellum had its freak shows. And one of the things they supposedly had was wrestling and boxing matches between blind people in some back room somewhere.[16]

Samuel Charters also found references to Jefferson having wrestled: "At first singing wasn't enough. He wrestled for money in Dallas theaters. Since he was blind, he could be billed as a novelty wrestler. He weighed nearly 250 pounds."[17]

When the 1920 census was taken, Lemon Jefferson was back living near where he had grown up. The census records for Freestone County, Precinct 5, taken on January 9 and 10, 1920, show Lemon Jefferson, as his name is now spelled, sharing lodgings with a married couple named Banks and a boarder, Mary Smith. The first name of the head of the household is nearly illegible, probably "Nit" or "Kit," while his middle initial, C, and last name, Banks, are clearly written. Alex van der Tuuk clarifies: "This is Issac C. Banks, Jefferson's half-brother. The 1930 and 1940 census for Lula Banks give his entries as well."[18] Identified as a twenty-nine-year-old mulatto, Issac was born in Texas and worked as a farmer. His wife, Lula B. Banks, was an unemployed nineteen-year-old black woman. Jefferson's entry begins, "Jefferson, Lemon, half-brother," suggesting that he was related to the head of the household. And here, for the first time in the public record, Lemon Jefferson's profession is described as "Musician." A subsequent entry in the 1920 Freestone

County census records shows the rest of the Jefferson family living in another household: Alex and Classie Jefferson, and their three daughters, Mary, twenty; Sebe, seventeen; and Gussie M., fifteen.[19]

Around 1923 Jefferson married a woman named Roberta— neighbors in Wortham remembered her as mousy and quiet—and within a couple of years they had a son. But according to pianist Sam Price, who knew him in Deep Ellum in the 1920s, becoming a husband didn't soften Blind Lemon's personality:

> Blind Lemon Jefferson would start out from South Dallas about eleven o'clock in the morning and follow the railroad tracks to Deep Ellum, and he'd get to the corner where Central Tracks crossed Elm about one or two in the afternoon, and he'd sing and play guitar until about ten o'clock at night. Then he'd start back home. He was a little chunky fellow who wasn't only a singer. He was a bootlegger, and when he'd get back home he had such a sensitive ear. He didn't want his wife to drink. Well, when he'd go away she'd take two or three drinks out of the bottle and she'd think he wouldn't know it. But he'd take the bottle when he came home and say, "Hey, how you doin' baby? How'd we do today?" [She'd respond] "Nobody bought no whiskey." Well, he'd take the bottle and shake it, and he could hear that there were two or three drinks missing. And what he'd do, he'd beat the hell out of her for that.[20]

By then Blind Lemon was so heavy that he had to play with his guitar perched atop his stomach, the upper bout just under his chin. His friend Alex Moore sighed: "He was the eatin'est man I ever saw."[21] The best-known photo of Jefferson, an autographed Paramount publicity shot, depicts an inscrutable Buddha-like man cradling an inexpensive round-hole acoustic on his lap. The fact that the ornate penmanship is nearly identical to that on Blind Blake's Paramount promo photo from the same era suggests that it was signed by somebody other than Lemon.

Women reportedly fawned over him. Blues singer Victoria Spivey, who began recording in 1926, recalled in a 1966 issue of *Record Research* that

Blind Lemon was a medium-size brownskin who kept himself neatly dressed. He was erect in posture, and his speech was lovely and direct to the word. He had no glasses when I first saw him. A young man who was very attentive to him acted as his guide. Although he was supposed to be completely blind, I still believe he could see a little bit. If he couldn't, he darn sure could feel his way 'round—the old wolf! Lemon never let his misfortune of sight press him. He could let you know that he was just as much a man as anybody. One of his most common expressions was "Don't play me cheap"—and most people liked him and respected him.[22]

Lead Belly also spent time with Blind Lemon Jefferson. The bluesmen met in Deep Ellum before World War I, and Lead Belly credited his one-time playing partner with teaching him single-string runs on guitar. The men played together at the Dallas train depot, as well as at house parties and on the streets. In 1944, Lead Belly recorded a twelve-string guitar instrumental called "Blind Lemon (Memorial Record)," introducing the piece by saying, "Now, when me and Blind Lemon Jefferson used to play around together in Dallas, Texas, I used to dance and he used to play this number for me to dance to." In "Silver City Bound," Lead Belly also sang of them traveling together:

> Silver City bound, I'm Silver City bound,
> I'm gonna tell my baby, I'm Silver City bound,
> Me and Blind Lemon, gonna ride on down.

Lead Belly's song goes on to quote Blind Lemon, saying he'd holler:

> Catch me by the hand, aw, baby,
> And lead me all through the land.[23]

Lead Belly met Jefferson before World War I, playing twelve-string guitar. "Him and I was buddies," Lead Belly said. "We used to play all up around Dallas, Texas." Courtesy Playboy Records and Books.

"Him and I was buddies," Lead Belly explained to Frederic Ramsey Jr. during his final recording session in September 1948.

> We used to play all up around Dallas, Texas, Fort Worth. We just get on
> the train. In them time we get on the 11 that run from Waco to Dallas,
> Corsicana, Waxahachie. From Dallas, then they had another one run
> to Fort Worth. I get Blind Lemon, we get our two guitars, and we'll just
> ride anything. We didn't have to pay no money in them time. We get
> on the train, we ride, take us anywhere we want to go. We'll just get
> on, and the conductor says, "Boys, just sit down. You all going to play
> music?" We told him, "Yas. We just out collectin' money"—that's what
> we want to have, some money, you know. And so we sit down and we'd
> turn the seats over, and he'd sit in front of me and I'd sit down there
> and start. Got a Silver City out there too. We always go through Silver
> City. And when we get on the bus we're Silver City bound first. A lot
> of pretty gals out there, and that's what we're lookin' for. You know we
> like for women to be around, 'cause when women around, that brings
> mens, and we get money. 'Cause when you get out there, the women
> get to drinkin' and not thinkin'. They just fall all up on you and, boy,
> that makes us feel good and we tear them guitars all to pieces.[24]

T-Bone Walker also claimed to have worked with the heavyset singer in the sweat-soaked black Stetson. "I used to lead Blind Lemon Jefferson around playing and passing the cup, take him from one beer joint to another," he reminisced in a 1947 article in *Record Changer* magazine. "I liked hearing him play. He would sing like nobody's business. He was a friend of my father's. People used to crowd around so you couldn't see him."[25] In 1972, Walker elaborated further for *Living Blues*: "My whole family was crazy about him. He'd come over every Sunday and sit with us and play his guitar, and they sang and they had a few drinks. You know, at that time they were drinking corn whiskey and home brew, things like that. 'Cause you couldn't buy any whiskey unless it was bootleg in those days."[26]

Mance Lipscomb, a fine Texas songster who played a haunting pocketknife slide version of Blind Lemon's "Jack O' Diamond Blues," told Glen Myers about seeing Jefferson in Deep Ellum in

1917: "He was a big stout fella, husky fella, loud voice. And he played dance songs and never did much church song. I ain't never known him to play a church song. He's a blues man. He had a tin cup, wired on the neck of his guitar. And when you pass to give him something, why he'd thank you. But he would never take no pennies. You could drop a penny in there and he'd know the sound. He'd take and throw it away. I liked Blind Lemon Jefferson's playing and his kind of blues."[27]

During the mid-1920s Paramount Records customers wrote in requesting 78s of country-blues artists. There are two versions of how Blind Lemon was signed to the label. In one, Sam Price, a black pianist who probably worked in R. J. Ashford's Dallas music store, reportedly recommended Jefferson to Paramount. Another account holds that Paramount recording director Arthur C. Laibly heard Jefferson playing on a Dallas street. Since the label didn't have any recording facilities in the South during this time, Jefferson was transported to Chicago to record. He attended his first session in late 1925 or early 1926, cutting two religious songs under the pseudonym Deacon L. J. Bates. The disc—"I Want to Be Like Jesus in My Heart" backed with "All I Want Is That Pure Religion"—was withheld until after several of his blues records came out.[28]

At his next session, in March 1926, Jefferson worked under his own name and played the blues. The date yielded a pair of 78s unlike anything heard before: "Booster Blues" backed with "Dry Southern Blues," and "Got the Blues" backed with "Long Lonesome Blues." In a newspaper ad, Paramount Records claimed, "Here's a real old-fashioned blues by a real old-fashioned blues singer—Blind Lemon Jefferson from Dallas. This 'Booster Blues' and 'Dry Southern Blues' on the reverse side are two of Blind Lemon's old-time tunes. With his singing, he strums his guitar in real southern style—makes it talk, in fact."[29] A month later, the second 78 was issued. Even though these records were raw and uncompromising, sales were strong. The fact

Jefferson's first blues 78 paired "Booster Blues" with "Dry Southern Blues."
Courtesy Roger Misiewicz and Helge Thygesen.

that Paramount's innovative mail-order service could penetrate into rural communities without local record dealers certainly helped.

Mayo Williams remembered that during the Chicago recording sessions, Blind Lemon was "just as cool and calm and collected as any artist I've ever seen."[30] Jefferson cut more 78s in May 1926, including "Black Horse Blues," "Corinna Blues," and two takes of the old gambling song "Jack O' Diamond Blues," played with a slide. In July or August, he recorded "Beggin' Back" and "Old Rounders Blues." He returned again in October to record eight more songs, including

"Broke and Hungry," "Stocking Feet Blues," "Booger Rooger Blues," and "Rabbit Foot Blues." For sheer hard-luck poetry, it was hard to beat "That Black Snake Moan":

> *Ohhh, ain't got no mama now,*
> *Ohhh, ain't got no mama now,*
> *She told me late last night, you don't need no mama no how.*
>
> *Ohhh, that must have been a bed bug, baby, a chinch can't bite that*
>   *hard,*
> *Ohhh, that must been a bed bug, honey, a chinch can't bite that*
>   *hard,*
> *Asked my sugar for fifty cents, she said, "Lemon, ain't a child in*
>   *the yard."*[31]

A "chinch" was a flying insect commonly found in rice and corn fields.

In 1927, Blind Lemon Jefferson moonlighted for OKeh Records. OKeh's Polk Brockman and T. J. Rockwell arranged for the session, which was to be held in Atlanta on March 14 and 15. They escorted Jefferson to the Dallas train station and arranged to follow him on a later train. When Jefferson was late showing up in Atlanta, Brockman asked where he'd been. Jefferson responded that he'd never been to Shreveport and had stopped off to "see" the town. "He got around remarkably well for a blind man," Brockman told *Living Blues*.[32] Asked if Jefferson had misgivings about recording for another label, Brockman responded, "No, he was ready."[33] In all, Jefferson recorded eight songs for OKeh. The label issued a 78 featuring what would become two of his most-covered songs, a new version of "Black Snake Moan" and "Match Box Blues," which borrowed its most famous line from an earlier Ma Rainey song. When Paramount protested the 78, OKeh withheld the other six songs from release.

The following month, Jefferson was back in Chicago recording for Paramount. His April sessions produced two takes of "Match

For sheer hard-luck poetry, it's hard to beat the lyrics of "That Black Snake Moan." Courtesy Alex van der Tuuk.

Box Blues," probably intended to compete with the OKeh release, and a single take of "Easy Rider Blues," which may have been a variation of the unreleased "My Easy Rider" he'd recorded for OKeh. In late April, Jefferson, sans guitar, was accompanied by pianist George Perkins on "Rising High Water Blues." He did play guitar on "Weary Dogs Blues" and "Right of Way Blues." In May, Paramount brought in Perkins again for "Teddy Bear Blues" and "Black Snake Dream Blues." The engineer had Blind Lemon play foot-tap accompaniment for the good-time "Hot Dogs," which came out credited to "Blind Lemon Jefferson and His Feet." Jefferson also cut a gospel side, "He Arose from the Dead." The Paramount release resurrected the "Deacon L. J. Bates" pseudonym for this recording, which also came out on Herwin credited to "Elder J. C. Brown."

During the fall of 1927, Blind Lemon Jefferson recorded ten more songs for Paramount Records, including his haunting and beloved "See That My Grave Is Kept Clean." In 1991 I asked B.B. King which Blind Lemon Jefferson song he'd recommend. King closed his eyes, took a deep breath, and gently began singing,

> *See that my grave be kept clean,*
> *See that my grave be kept clean,*
> *See that my grave be kept clean,*
> *See da-da-da-da-da-da.*

"That's one of them," King said. "Lightnin' Hopkins did it, and many people have done it since. But that's where it came from." He then resumed singing,

> *It's long road ain't got no end,*
> *Long road ain't got no end,*
> *Long road ain't . . .*[34]

Jefferson's performances on his 1926–27 records are among his very best, but the original Paramount pressings suffered from inferior sound. In 1986, Nick Perls, owner of Yazoo Records, gathered the best-surviving copies he could find of these early 78s to assemble his sonically superior two-record vinyl set *King of the Country Blues,* now available on CD. Perls wrote:

> I really put in a lot of work trying to get the best copies to dub and do a lot of de-clicking. So I'm pretty proud of the sound. As Blind Lemon's career progresses, his sound gets better but his performances worse. So I went for the early stuff when the Paramount engineers were so scared of his big voice that they jacked down the levels and subsequently got a poor signal-to-noise ratio even for the best copies. By

contrast, Blind Blake's fidelity was better because his voice was less powerful than Blind Lemon's, and so Paramount could keep up the levels. And unlike Blind Lemon Jefferson, Blake's accompaniments got more adventurous as his career went along.[35]

Blind Lemon Jefferson's 78s made an immediate impact upon musicians, especially country artists. "Up 'til then," recalled Roscoe Holcomb, a white mountain musician from Kentucky, "the blues were only inside me. Blind Lemon was the first to 'let out' the blues."[36] Asked why Blind Lemon's records became popular among white buyers, Steve James responded, "They could understand what he was saying, and his subject matter was sometimes funny. To poor white people there would be a bond of commonality, and to town whites it was what they expected a blues singer to sing about—his lucky charm, his prison sentence, his fat girlfriend, and that kind of stuff. This was unlike someone like Skip James, who really lost them coming out of the gate by singing about 'You're gonna die, it's gonna hurt, it's gonna be pretty soon.' Lemon was perceived a lot as old-timey, and that helped too."[37]

While Lemon's greatest appeal was his field-holler-powerful vocals, his idiosyncratic guitar playing certainly set him apart. For starters, his fingerpicking approach wasn't always governed by the steady bass beat and deliberate bar structure common to most bluesmen. He was a master of the open pentatonic scale, and several of his stronger pieces plied only the first, altered third, fifth, altered seventh, and octave. "He had something in his phrasing that's so funny," described B.B. King.

> He had a way of double-time playing. Say, like, one-two-three-four, and then he'd go [in double-time] one-two-three-four, one-two-three-four. And the time was still right there, but double time. And then he could come out of it so easy. And then when he would resolve something, it was done so well. But he'd come out of it so smooth. His touch is different from anybody on the guitar—still is. I've practiced, I tried, I did everything, and still I could never come out with the sound as he

did. He was majestic, and he played just a regular little six-string guitar with a little round hole. It was unbelievable to hear him play. And the way he played with his rhythm patterns, he was way before his time, in my opinion.[38]

Mike Bloomfield described Jefferson as "really a great player, very fast, very strange. Blind Lemon didn't play with a beat—you couldn't dance to his music."[39] Steve James has a different take:

People say Lemon had no meter, but he had fabulous meter—he just stretched the verses out. It's a Texas thing; he basically did the same thing that Lightnin' Hopkins did on his Gold Star stuff. For instance, sometimes he had a lick that was a bar longer than the twelve-bar structure dictated. Sometimes he'd do as many of these fast single-note

Paramount's ad copy for "Long Lonesome Blues" describes how Jefferson, feeling suicidal, "trudges mournfully to the riverside" and "looks at the swirling water"—quite a feat for a blind man. Courtesy Tim Gracyk.

lines as he wanted to before going back to the chord, and then he'd strum. Other times he'd do some rolls à la Blind Blake—he had a tremendous thumb—and then he'd break his bass pattern. Sometimes he would do an alternating bass line, or he'd just smack a monotonic bass line and then walk boogie lines.

He had beautiful arrangements where he'd walk a bass line up against a descending melody, almost like classical or ragtime counterpoint. I don't want to compare his playing harmonically to Blind Blake, but like Blind Blake he was a very economical player. He could do some stunning licks, and he was obviously in real command of the fingerboard. He could do so much business below the fifth fret, it's unbelievable. Like "Bad Luck," one of my favorite Lemon tunes, is a stunning performance in the key of C, where he actually sets up a treble figure and changes the bass line over it as he changes chords. Then he winds up the turnaround on the V, and the resolution of the song is this really beautiful counterpoint line.

Lemon played in a lot of different keys, and he recorded a number of pieces in open-G tuning. And there's a difference between the way he plays in E and C. The way he plays in A reminds me of Funny Paper Smith and Texas Alexander, with that spread A chord where you bridge the top four strings on the second fret and use the pinky up on the fifth fret. While some people have said that things like "Black Snake Moan" were played with a flat pick, I'm not sure that's true. I think he just played with his thumb and finger and was able to do that. And it sounds to me that he played some of his denser fingerpicking stuff with his thumb and two fingers.[40]

Stefan Grossman believes Blind Lemon was both flat-picker and fingerpicker:

His "Black Horse Blues" was almost like Rev. Gary Davis, this intricate Carolina picking that's definitely done with his fingers. But then there's that whole slew of blues in C, which are definitely imitations of Jimmie Rodgers, the big star of American music at that time. When Blind Lemon plays the bass parts on those songs, it sounds like a flat pick. Then when he takes his breaks, you don't hear any fingerpicking. On the early Lonnie Johnson solo sides, when he's doing single-string runs, every once in a while you start to hear the bass come in, so you know he's using fingers. I would almost bet that Lemon was using a flat pick. It makes sense: Here's a guy on the street corners, singing the songs that people want to hear.[41]

In the Paramount publicity photo, Jefferson appears to be wearing a white thumbpick.

While details of Jefferson's day-to-day life are nearly nonexistent, his lyrics suggest that he enjoyed traveling. In "Rambler Blues," for instance, recorded in September 1927, he sang of leaving home, where he "left his baby crying," and of wanting to catch the number nine train. If someone takes his girl while he's gone, so be it:

If you take my rider, I can't get mad with you,
If you take my rider, I can't get mad with you,
Just like you're takin' mine, I'll take someone else's too.

He concludes the song with a lament to his women troubles:

I got a girl in Texas, I got a brown in Tennessee,
I got a brown in Texas, one in Tennessee,
Lord, but that brown in Chicago have put that jinx bug on me.[42]

In its ad copy for the song, Paramount conveyed the image of a man on the move: "Will he ever come back to his home and his sweetie? There he goes, roaming and rambling 'round the country—seems to be happy if you give him his guitar and a good smoke. His Pullman car is his palace and he seems to have a lower berth, with a through ticket wherever he wants to go."[43]

Judging from reported sightings, Jefferson spent considerable time on the road. Sam Price remembered him playing boogie-woogie and using the term "booger rooger" as far back as 1917, when he heard him playing in Waco, Texas. Hobart Smith, a white musician in Saltville, Virginia, recalled seeing him before World War I: "It was along about that time that Blind Lemon Jefferson came through," Smith explained to *Sing Out!*, "and he stayed around there about a month. He stayed with the other colored fellows and they worked on the railroad there. He'd just sing and play to entertain the men in the work camp. I think that right about there I started on the guitar."[44] Jefferson's influence resounded in Smith's renditions of "Six White Horses" and "Graveyard Blues."

Albert King, born in Mississippi in 1924, claimed to have seen him in Arkansas. "The first bluesman I saw was Blind Lemon Jefferson," he told Dan Forte.

> Later I heard him on records, but I used to see him in these parks, like on Saturday afternoons in these little country towns around Forest City, Arkansas. We'd work till noon on Saturdays, and then my stepdad would hook up the wagon, and sometimes my sister and I and the other kids could go to town. This one particular day he was there playing acoustic guitar, and he had his cup. He sounded something like that folk singer, Richie Havens—something on that order. He had a crowd of people around him, and we'd put nickels in his cup, and he'd play a song.[45]

Lightnin' Hopkins recalled seeing Blind Lemon play at a Baptist picnic in Buffalo, Texas. Others claimed to have watched him play with a band in Alabama. One eyewitness told Gayle Dean Wardlow that "folks wouldn't go to bed at night" when Jefferson played in Minden, Louisiana.[46]

Howlin' Wolf remembered seeing Blind Lemon in Mississippi in 1926, the same year he first saw Charley Patton. According to Gayle Dean Wardlow, Jefferson enjoyed a huge popularity in the Delta, where he was mimicked by nearly every player who had the skill to do so. Ralph Lembo, a Sicilian-born record company talent scout who owned a furniture store in Itta Bena, Mississippi, paid Jefferson's train fare from Chicago and arranged for him to play in his store. "He charged customers 25 cents admission for a view of the artist," reported Wardlow and Stephen Calt in their Charley Patton biography, *King of the Delta Blues*.

> Despite advanced fanfare (prior to the performance, he had paraded Jefferson about town on a wagon), the promotional stunt backfired,

Paramount Records' "Booster Blues" advertisement ran in the April 3, 1926, issue of the *Chicago Defender,* a popular African American newspaper. Courtesy Alex van der Tuuk.

and after three hours of playing music Jefferson had grown so dissatisfied by the receipts Lembo collected that he refused to continue.
Another financial dispute skewered his scheduled appearance (probably the same evening) at Itta Bena's Rolling Wall High School: "They
had a big dance there and Lemon come in and play, and they was
chargin' 75 cents to come in," David Edwards recalled. "That was a lot
of money then, and they couldn't get him to play for that 75 cents."[47]

Lembo's attempt to pair Blind Lemon Jefferson and Charley Patton
at a recording session also failed.

Reverend Rubin Lacy, another Delta bluesman, met Jefferson
during a March 1928 Paramount session in Chicago. Blind Lemon
was there to record "Piney Woods Money Mama," which was issued
with a special yellow-and-white picture label bearing his photograph and the legend "Blind Lemon Jeffersons' Birthday Record."
Lacy told David Evans in 1966,

> I invited Blind Lemon to come to Itta Bena and visit me, which he did,
> and we played in the theater in Greenwood and the theater in Moor-
> head together. And he stayed around there, I think, a week or two with
> me, played first one place, then another, 'til he had to go back again to
> make another record, because he had to make one a month. Directly
> after that he just died, I think, overnight. Some say he was just too
> fat. I know one thing, if you go to sleep here in the house at night, you
> could hear him snoring I don't know how far.
>
> He was kind. Wouldn't play a guitar on Sunday for nobody—I don't
> care what you offered him. I seed a fellow offer him $20 to play him
> one song one morning. Two men walked up and said, "We'll give you
> $10 apiece if you'll play 'Blues come through Texas loping like a mule.'"
> Shook his head. He say, "I couldn't play it if you give me $200. I need
> the money, but I couldn't play it. My mother always taught me not to
> play on Sunday for nobody. Today is Sunday." And I spoke and said,
> "I'll play it!" I might as well play it on Sunday as play it on a Monday.[48]

Ishmon Bracey, a Delta musician who made his recording
debut for Victor in 1928, also saw Jefferson in Greenwood. "Blind
Lemon used to come to Greenwood every fall and let me follow him

around," Bracey told Gayle Dean Wardlow. "He didn't trust them other people. He carried a pearl-handled .44, and he could shoot the head off a chicken. And he couldn't see nary a lick. Just did it from the sound he heard. He broke time, but he was good, I'm telling you. He'd be down there in the fall when people's pickin' cotton. Everybody wanted to see Lemon. I could second him, but a lot of guitar players couldn't stay with him."[49]

In an interview with *Living Blues* founding editor Jim O'Neal, Houston Stackhouse, a musician from Wesson, Mississippi, remembered seeing Jefferson around this same time:

Blind Lemon Jefferson's only 78 on OKeh Records coupled "Match Box Blues" and "Black Snake Moan." He recorded different takes of these songs for Paramount Records, adding foot stomps to both new versions of "Match Box Blues." Courtesy Roger Misiewicz and Helge Thygesen.

1928, I believe it was, when I saw him. He came to Crystal Springs and playin' for some little show for a doctor, you know, just sellin' medicine there. He was the onliest one [in the show] playin' the guitar at that time. They had it in Freetown there at the colored school. There's plenty of people there. It was a big school, and it's just crowded all indoors—people couldn't get in to see him. They had to bring him out up to the front, on the porch. They come to see him. He was a big name then. . . . He played many a song there that night. Yeah, he played great. He played that "Wonder Will His Matchbox Hold His Clothes" and all that. And so Tommy Johnson came down that night. He just stood around and looked at him.[50]

Stackhouse, who learned music from Tommy Johnson and his brothers, recalled that Tommy Johnson knew some of Jefferson's repertoire and that the two bluesmen played together: "They was runnin' around. He'd come down, he'd say, 'Well, me and that old Blind Lemon had it,' you know, some nights like that. Say, 'We got together. We balled awhile.' Yeah, Blind Lemon was popular through that country."[51] Another witness reported seeing him at the Parchman Farm penitentiary on the Fourth of July.

Near the end of his recording career, Jefferson tended to rework the same musical themes. He continued to emphasize single-note runs, but some of his arrangements became less harmonically interesting. There's marked progression in Blind Lemon's material too. His earliest work tended to be traditional material or direct reworkings of field hollers and work songs. "See That My Grave Is Kept Clean," for instance, was based on a folk melody known throughout the South; "Corinna Blues" was partially derived from "See See Rider." But by early 1928, Jefferson's lyrics were becoming more thematic. For instance, he seemed to have a special concern for the fate of prison inmates, as evidenced by his first recordings in 1928, "Blind Lemon's Penitentiary Blues" and "'Lectric Chair Blues." That February he recorded "Prison Cell Blues," and July found him singing "Lockstep Blues" and "Hangman's Blues," both of which he recut before the year's end. In July, he also covered Leroy Carr's big hit, "How Long How Long," complete with piano accompaniment. The 78's flip side featured a Tampa Red performance.

Some of Jefferson's most compelling compositions of 1929, the last year of his life, were packed with sexual metaphor and fantasy. "I don't like me plenty of women," he sang in "Saturday Night Spender Blues," "but man, I likes them wild." He portrayed women with terms such as "rider," "pigmeat," "brown," "dirty mistreaters," or even "fair-made" yet "cunning as a squirrel." His "Black Snake Moan No. 2" began with the announcement, "Well, folks, Lemon is yet lookin' for his black snake mama." And few could miss the underlying meaning of his "Bakershop Blues," cut at his final session on September 24, 1929:

> *I'm crazy 'bout my light bread and my pigmeat on the side,*
> *I said I'm crazy about my light bread, my pigmeat on the side,*
> *But I taste your jelly roll, and I'd be satisfied.*[52]

In between his sessions and rambles, Jefferson stayed in Dallas or at his kitchenette apartment on Chicago's South Side. His financial success was such that he could afford to travel in a chauffeur-driven Ford and at one time had $1,500 in the bank.

Within a few months of his final session, Blind Lemon was dead and gone. For decades, mystery surrounded the circumstances of his demise. Mike Bloomfield expressed one popular version: "In 1929, he froze to death in the gutter trying to get from one part of Chicago to another. His chauffeur had split. One story has it that his guitar froze right to his hand. Very odd."[53] Others say he was poisoned by a jealous lover. Rube Lacy speculated that "he just died overnight from being too fat, just smothered to death."[54] In May 1930, the duo Walter and Byrd recorded "Wasn't It Sad about Lemon" for Paramount, singing: "'Twas on the streets of Chicago was where poor Lemon fell." On the flip side of this memorial 78,

Rev. Emmett Dickinson's "Death of Blind Lemon" eulogized: "Let us pause a moment and look at the life of our beloved Lemon Jefferson who was born blind. It is in many respects like that of our Lord, Jesus Christ. Like him, unto the age of thirty he was unknown, and also like him in a short space of a little over three years his name and works were known in every home."[55]

In recent years, as Alex van der Tuuk explains, new details on Jefferson's demise have emerged:

> In 2006, Jefferson's death certificate was finally discovered, listing his name as George Jefferson, as his landlady, who acted as the informant, recalled his name. She seemed unaware of his musical stardom, as his occupation was listed as "blind." Jefferson, as has been reported for so many years, did indeed die in the streets of Chicago, in the 3700 block of South Rhodes Avenue, close to the address of his landlady, with whom he resided at 3754 South Rhodes Avenue. According to the death certificate, Jefferson probably died of chronic myocarditis, although no medical examination had taken place. Jefferson's body had to be taken back to Texas.[56]

The *Wortham Journal* reported his death in its January 3, 1930, issue. The article headlined "Lemon Jefferson Dies in Chicago" offered these details:

> Lemon Jefferson, 45, a blind Negro who was reared in Wortham and the community, died of heart failure and was shipped to Wortham for burial, arriving here on Christmas Eve. Lemon was on the streets of Wortham almost every day singing songs of his composition and playing his guitar, until some two years ago he was visiting Dallas and a phonograph record scout picked him up and carried him to Chicago where he has sung many of his Negro songs for a record company, and it is said that his royalties from records has gained to a considerable sum. The last time he visited Wortham before his death, he came in a big automobile, his own, and was accompanied by a chauffeur.[57]

More than two hundred people, black and white, watched as Blind Lemon Jefferson was lowered into the ground of the Wortham

Negro Cemetery. Perhaps a few of those in attendance recalled his famous lyric:

> *Well, there's one kind favor I ask of you,*
> *Well, there's one kind favor I ask of you,*
> *Lord, it's one kind favor I'll ask of you,*
> *See that my grave is kept clean.*[58]

For years it wasn't, but in 1967 the Texas State Historical Association provided a historical marker. Steve James describes the site:

> The cemetery is on Highway 14, a couple of miles east of Wortham. You have to park your car, open a cattle gate, and walk through somebody's property to get to it. It's a quiet place on a little hillock that overlooks this really beautiful east Texas Brazos bottomland. There's a controversy about where Lemon's grave is, because a lot of people said that the monument wasn't placed over his grave. Lemon was said to have been buried just inside the gate; however, Uel Davis says that the gate used to be on the other side when they buried him. So maybe the monument's actually on the opposite side of the cemetery.[59]

In 1997, a proper headstone was placed over Jefferson's grave.

Through the decades, Blind Lemon Jefferson's style has reverberated through many players—Son House, Alger "Texas" Alexander, Ramblin' Thomas, Lead Belly, T-Bone Walker, Lightnin' Hopkins, John Lee Hooker, J. B. Lenoir, Johnny Shines, Mance Lipscomb, B.B. King, Steve James, and the list goes on. Western swing's most enduring hit, Bob Wills and his Texas Playboys' 1939 "Swing Blues No. 1," borrowed a verse from "Long Lonesome Blues." Jefferson's 78s of "Match Box Blues," "That Black Snake Moan," and "See That My Grave Is Kept Clean" were covered by Southern musicians for decades. And today "Match Box Blues" is a rock standard, with notable covers by Carl Perkins, the Beatles, Bob Dylan, John Fogerty, Taj Mahal, and Jesse Ed Davis. For sheer spirit and vibe, though, it's unlikely that anyone will ever surpass Blind Lemon Jefferson's original recordings.

Cordially Yours
Blind Blake

BLIND BLAKE

*King of Ragtime
Blues Guitar*

DURING THE MID-1920S, strong sales of 78s by Papa Charlie Jackson and Blind Lemon Jefferson led Paramount Records to sign Blind Blake, a swinging, sophisticated guitarist whose warm, relaxed voice was a far cry from harsh country blues. Some of Blake's 78s cast him as a jivey hipster sitting in with jazzmen, while on others he walked the long, lonely road to the gallows. The man with the "famous piano-sounding guitar" is still regarded as the unrivaled master of ragtime blues fingerpicking.[1]

"Lord have mercy, was he sophisticated!" says Jorma Kaukonen, who helped introduce Blake's guitar style to rock audiences during the 1970s. "He would have been sophisticated in any era. I really like the completeness of his piano-style playing, his left- and right-hand moves. He could play a complete band arrangement by himself. That appealed to the lone-wolf mentality that I aspired to when I was learning his songs. Later on, it gave me depth for playing double-guitar and piano-guitar stuff with other people. It taught me a lot about putting music together."[2]

The only known photograph of Blind Blake shows him fingerpicking a small-bodied guitar, possibly a Chicago-made Harmony. Courtesy Helge Thygesen.

Blind Blake

E have all heard expressions of people "singing in the rain" or "laughing in the face of adversity," but we never saw such a good example of it, until we came upon the history of Blind Blake. Born in Jacksonville, in sunny Florida, he seems to have absorbed some of the sunny atmosphere — disregarding the fact that nature had cruelly denied him a vision of outer things. He could not see the things that others saw—but he had a better gift. A gift of an inner vision, that allowed him to see things more beautiful. The pictures that he alone could see made him long to express them in some way — so he turned to music. He studied long and earnestly — listening to talented pianists and guitar players, and began to gradually draw out harmonious tunes to fit every mood. Now that he is recording exclusively for Paramount, the public has the benefit of his talent, and agrees, as one body, that he has an unexplainable gift of making one laugh or cry as he feels, and sweet chords and tones that come from his talking guitar express a feeling of his mood.

Blind Blake's bio page in the 1927 promotional booklet *The Paramount Book of Blues.*
Courtesy of the author.

"Blind Blake is a great player, a great musical figure," echoes Ry Cooder. "In the years where he was on top, he was fabulous. Blind Blake just had a good touch. He played quietly, and he didn't hit the guitar too hard. He had a nice feeling for syncopation. He's from down there in the Geechie country, and all those people have a real nice roll to what they do. He was a hell of a good player, and he had a lick that was great. And Blind Blake played all over the place, with all kinds of people, including Johnny Dodds, which is just way too much for me."[3]

Besides his music and session details, not much is known of Blind Blake. His single surviving photograph shows a dapper bantamweight in a neatly pressed three-piece suit and bow tie, fingerpicking a small guitar beneath closed eyes and a frozen grin. With its deep body and distinctive bridge, the guitar in the photo is likely a Chicago-made Harmony, a good guitar back then. *The Paramount Book of Blues* offered these insights:

> We have all heard expressions of people "singing in the rain" or "laughing in the face of adversity," but we never saw such a good example of it, until we came upon the history of Blind Blake. Born in Jacksonville, in sunny Florida, he seems to have absorbed some of the sunny atmosphere—disregarding the fact that nature had cruelly denied him a vision of outer things. He could not see the things that others saw—but he had a better gift. A gift of an inner vision, that allowed him to see things more beautiful. The pictures that he alone could see made him long to express them in some way—so he turned to music. He studied long and earnestly—listening to talented pianists and guitar players, and began to gradually draw out harmonious tunes to fit every mood. Now that he is recording exclusively for Paramount, the public has the benefit of his talent, and agrees, as one body, that he has an unexplainable gift of making one laugh or cry as he feels, and sweet chords and tones that come from his talking guitar express a feeling of his mood.[4]

Paramount's ads emphasized Blake's unparalleled guitar playing: "He accompanies himself with that snappy guitar playing, like only Blind Blake can do" read the ad copy for "Bad Feeling Blues." The company claimed that "Blind Blake and his trusty guitar do themselves proud" on "Rumblin' & Ramblin' Boa Constrictor Blues," while "Wabash Rag" was "aided by his happy guitar."[5]

Some believe Blind Blake was born Arthur Phelps, but during the record "Papa Charlie and Blind Blake Talk about It—Part 1," Papa Charlie Jackson asks him, "What is your right name?" Blake responds, "My name is Arthur Blake."[6] The name on the copyrights for "C. C. Pill Blues" and "Panther Squall Blues" is Arthur "Blind" Blake, which strengthens the case for Blake being his given name. He had a pronounced Southern accent and reportedly worked in south Georgia, in Kentucky, along the East Coast, and in Bristol, Tennessee, before landing in Chicago.

On his death certificate, Blake's place of birth was listed as Newport News, Virginia, and 1896 was entered as his date of birth. "No matter where Blake was from, he ranks as a musical curiosity," wrote Steve Calt and Woody Mann in the liners for Yazoo's *Blind Blake* collection. "His records betray no basic musical orientation, and it's anyone's guess as to whether blues, guitar instrumentals, or even pop ditties were his original specialty. How he actually made his livelihood as a performer is another enigma. While most blind guitarists were soloists who used the helter-skelter phrasing of the street dancer, Blake's blues phrasing had the strictness of a dance or band musician. It is likely that ensemble playing (perhaps with a jazz band) had a real impact on his music."[7]

Blind Blake made his first records for Paramount during the summer of 1926, playing solo guitar behind Leola B. Wilson's lazy vaudeville blues. "Mayo Williams, the Paramount scout, says that Blind Blake was sent up from Jacksonville by a dealer," reports blues researcher Gayle Dean Wardlow. "That's how he first got on record,

Blake energized his first solo release, "West Coast Blues," with spirited asides such as "Whoop that thing" and "I'm gonna satisfy you if I can." Courtesy Roger Misiewicz and Helge Thygesen.

and his records sold very, very well."[8] Blake showed nerves of steel his first time before the recording horn at Chicago's Marsh Laboratories, playing outstanding solos on Wilson's "Dying Blues" and "Ashley St. Blues." A month later Paramount cast him as a solo artist. "Early Morning Blues" was a grim "leaving blues." Blind Blake injected the 78's flip side, the brilliant "West Coast Blues," with spoken asides such as "Whoop that thing" and "I'm gonna satisfy you if I can."

Blake's releases influenced other blues guitarists, such as William Moore, who patterned his Paramount 78 of "Old Country Rock" on "West Coast Blues." Reverend Gary Davis likewise studied Blake's 78s. "The guitar was being played like a piano in almost all the areas of America except the Delta," explains Stefan Grossman, "meaning that the left hand was literally doing that boom-chick, boom-chick pattern. Blake was able to use his right-hand thumb to syncopate it more, like a Charleston. He was very, very rhythmic and incredibly fast—I don't know anyone who can get to that speed. That's Blake's real claim to fame, because his chord progressions are nothing fancy. But the thumb work is fantastic, and what he's doing with his right hand set him apart from everyone. Reverend Gary Davis said Blake had a 'sportin' right hand.' Davis took that and got into even more complicated modes."[9]

"I suspect Blind Blake was a three-finger picker," offers Jorma Kaukonen, "and I have a sneaking suspicion he wore picks, because he had such a snappy, percussive sound and he's not popping the strings the way bare-finger players do. His favorite keys were C, G, and E, although I'm pretty sure he could play in any of them if he wanted to."[10]

At his next session, October 1926, Blake balanced down-and-out blues songs with the good-time hokum of "Too Tight" and "Come on Boys Let's Do That Messin' Around," which has an early example of a scatted solo in a blues song. He flexed his guitar prowess on his next 78, "Skeedle Loo Doo Blues" and the double-time sections of "Stonewall Street Blues." Paramount summoned Blake and pianist Jimmy Blythe to Leola Wilson's November session, which produced a pair of fine 78s. Less than six months after his entry into the record biz, Blake was playing behind the great Ma Rainey on

"Morning Hour Blues," "Little Low Mamma Blues," and "Grievin' Hearted Blues."[11]

During the spring of 1927, Blake was accompanied by a kazoo player (possibly Dad Nelson) on "Buck-Town Blues." A bones percussionist was brought in for "Dry Bone Shuffle" and "That Will Never Happen No More." In October 1927 Blake cut the smoothly syncopated "Hey Hey Daddy Blues," "Sea Board Stomp" with its hip horn imitations, and the tour de force "Southern Rag." These performances suggest that he woodshedded on guitar during his half-year recording hiatus. "I'm goin' to give you some music they call the Geechie music now," Blake announced at the beginning of "Southern Rag," which he laced with images of planting rice, sugar cane, cotton, and peas. Some authors suggest that Blake slips into the Geechie and Gullah accents of Georgia's south Sea Islands during the track, but Wardlow disagrees: "I don't think he intentionally goes into the Geechie accent, but he was down from around that part of the country—South Carolina, Georgia, and Florida."[12]

In November 1927 Gus Cannon joined in on banjo for the minstrel tune "He's in the Jail House Now." During the 1950s Sam Charters asked Cannon for his memories of Blake. Cannon responded, "We drank so much whiskey! I'm telling you we drank more whiskey than a shop! And that boy would take me out with him at night and get me so turned around I'd be lost if I left his side. He could see more with his blind eyes than I with my two good ones."[13] Mayo Williams also reported that Blake would get drunk and fight.

In April 1928 two outstanding jazz musicians, Jimmy Bertrand and Johnny Dodds, joined Blind Blake for some session work in Chicago. Bertrand, a master drummer and xylophonist, was one of the city's top music teachers; his students included Lionel Hampton and Big Sid Catlett. Dodds had played and recorded with King

Blake's otherworldly "C. C. Pill Blues" featured Jimmy Bertrand on slide whistle and the great Johnny Dodds on clarinet. Courtesy Roger Misiewicz and Helge Thygesen.

Oliver, Louis Armstrong's Hot Five and Hot Seven, and Jelly Roll Morton. The jazzmen backed Blake on four remarkable sides, beginning with "Doggin' Me Mama Blues," on which Bertrand played a cartoony-sounding xylophone and made lots of spoken asides. "C. C. Pill Blues" featured Dodds on clarinet while Bertrand warbled away with a slide whistle. Their accompaniment on "Hot Potatoes" showcased Dodds's stellar clarinet solos and Bertrand's woodblock percussion and crazy slide whistling. The sophisticated "South Bound Rag" contained brilliant interplay between clarinet and xylophone while Blake kept spot-on time with his guitar. Of special interest to jazz fans, these recordings were reissued on the Broadway label credited to "Blind George Martin," as were a few other Blind Blake 78s. *Blues & Gospel Records, 1890-1943* reports that "South Bound Rag" was also released on the Australian XX label credited to "Gorgeous Weed and Stinking Socks"![14] Bertrand, Dodds, and Blake then accompanied Elzadie Robinson, a cabaret singer and former chorus girl from Logansport, Louisiana, on "Elzadie's Policy Blues" and "Pay Day Daddy Blues."

The following month Blake did more session work, playing guitar behind singer Bertha Henderson on four mournful songs. Her session's final selection, "Let Your Love Come Down," featured a skillful piano player adept with walking bass patterns and rocking right-hand solos. Just before the pianist's solo, Henderson said, "Oh, play it, Mister Blake!" so this is likely a rare example of Blind Blake stepping out on piano. Around this same time, Blake and pianist Tiny Parham provided spirited unison accompaniment to Daniel Brown's rendering of the religious song "Beulah Land." With his stately style of singing, Brown sounded like a throwback to the cylinder era—especially the 1890s recordings of George W. Johnson—and "Beulah Land" / "Now Is the Needy Time" would be his only 78.

Although Blind Blake was earning up to fifty dollars per Paramount side, Little Brother Montgomery claimed that the guitarist's regular source of income during the late 1920s came from playing South Side Chicago house rent parties. With its piano in the living room, Blake's apartment at 31st and Cottage Grove became a gathering place where Montgomery, Charlie Spand, Roosevelt Sykes, Tampa Red, Big Bill Broonzy, and other musicians could drink moonshine and jam blues. But not everyone could keep up. "I met Blind Blake in

Chicago," Ishmon Bracey told Gayle Dean Wardlow, "but I couldn't second him. He was too fast for me. Blind Blake, Tampa Red, Lonnie Johnson, and Scrapper Blackwell—all of them guitar players was buckin' one another. Blind Blake was too fast."[15]

Blake's September 1928 releases "Ramblin' Mama Blues," "Back Door Slam Blues," "Cold Hearted Mama Blues," and "Low Down Loving Gal" portray a man with bitter feelings toward women. His lyrics took a scarier turn on "Notoriety Woman Blues," during which he sang, "To keep her quiet I knocked her teeth out her mouth." By contrast, Blake's final recording that year, "Sweet Papa Low Down," was a bouncy Charleston with piano, cornet, Jimmy Bertrand's xylophone, and Blake's happy jiving.

The bluesman journeyed to Richmond, Indiana, in June 1929 for a series of sides with Alex Robinson on piano. A stand-out instrumental, "Slippery Rag," rocked the house with driving chords and mind-boggling solos. "Fightin' the Jug" reinforced his reputation for being a heavy drinker:

> *When I die, folks, without a doubt,*
> *When I die, folks, without a doubt,*
> *You won't have to do nothin' but pour me out.*[16]

Blind Blake was at the height of his powers on August 17, 1929, at what was to be his last great session. During the course of that Saturday in Richmond, he recorded several of his most enduring songs. While some of these songs were played in the bluesier keys of D and E, Blake relied on his favorite ragtime tuning, C, for "Georgia Bound." Blake went toe-to-toe with Charlie Spand, Detroit's premier piano boogieman, on "Hastings St.," named after a street in the city's old black section. I played this track for John Lee Hooker, who'd never heard it before, and he reacted by calling it "the real blues." He speculated that Blake must have lived in Detroit at some point, since Blake mentions a specific address, 169 Brady, during the song and then says, "Must be somethin' there very marvelous, mm, mm, mm. I believe it's somethin' that'll make you feel oh boy and how!"[17] "Yeah, Brady was right off of Gratiot," Hooker verified. "Detroit was jumpin' then, and Hastings Street was the best street in town. Everything you wanted was right there. Everything you didn't want was right there. It ain't no more now. It's a freeway now, called Chrysler Freeway. But that was a good street, a street known all over the world."[18]

Blake's next issued selection, "Diddie Wa Diddie," is a ragtime blues classic, each break a minor masterpiece. Blake masterfully heightened the song's rhythmic intensity by rushing to the root of a new chord an eighth note before the next downbeat. With its beautiful lines, harmonic chimes, and bluesy bends, "Police Dog Blues" likewise showcases his consummate guitarmanship. Jorma Kaukonen and Ry Cooder have both recorded inspired covers of this song. "Chump Man Blues" was another of the session's highlights. "Blind Blake was basically a ragtime guitar player," notes Stefan Grossman, "but then he had things like 'Chump Man Blues,' which is a blues in D. It's not as exciting as his playing in C or G, but it has an almost Bahaman, Joseph Spence sound."[19]

Blind Blake made a few more sides in Chicago later that summer and fall: a 78 featuring Tiny Parham or Aletha Dickerson on piano, the agile instrumentals "Guitar Chimes" and "Blind Arthur's Breakdown." "Papa Charlie and Blind Blake Talk about It," the first Blake 78 recorded at Paramount's new studio in Grafton, Wisconsin, joined two musical giants in a stuttering shuck-and-jive routine in January 1930. With its exaggerated vocals and Jackson's utilitarian banjo strums overwhelming the arrangement, the song wasn't far removed from old-time minstrelsy.

In late May 1930 Blake returned to Grafton, Wisconsin, to work as a session man for singer Irene Scruggs and to record four solo sides. At the first session, his playing sounded lackluster on

Scruggs's first selection, "Stingaree Man Blues." He picked up the tempo for "Itching Heel," navigating his parts with some of the skill that characterized his earlier recordings. The song no doubt struck a resonant chord among many women attached to bluesmen: "He don't do nothing but play on his old guitar / While I'm busting suds out in the white folks' yard."[20] Blake, in turn, responded to her verbal jabs with sped-up guitar parts. On May 28, Blake and Scruggs reunited for her "You've Got What I Want" and "Cherry Hill Blues." He managed to convey some of the old fire with energetic asides on the first song but turned in an uninspired performance on the second. In August Blake returned to the Grafton studio, cutting "Diddie Wa Diddie No. 2," "Hard Pushing Papa," "What a Low Down Place the Jailhouse Is," and "Ain't Gonna Do That No More." On these records, the sheen is mostly gone from Blind Blake's playing and singing. "When he started to drink too much—you can hear it towards the end—it just doesn't work anymore," observes Ry Cooder. "He's physically past it, because you've got to be sharp to sound that good."[21]

Blake was back in peak form for his circa November 1930 recording of "Righteous Blues," playing brilliant single-string and chord solos and slipping into a falsetto to suggest a woman's voice. Four months later, in his final appearance as a sideman, Blake accompanied Laura Rucker on "Fancy Tricks" but made no recordings of his own. Blake returned to Grafton in July 1931 to record the woeful two-part "Rope Stretchin' Blues," which tells the tale of a man who catches a stranger in his house, busts his head with a club, and winds up hanging for it.

Paramount Records' advertisement for 1927's "Wabash Rag" claims, "Blind Blake—aided by his happy guitar—will make you play this record over and over." Courtesy Alex van der Tuuk.

Blind Blake made his final six recordings between November 1931 and April 1932. For decades, no copy of "Dissatisfied Blues" / "Miss Emma Liza" was known to have survived, until one turned up at a North Carolina flea market in 2012; a second copy turned up in March 2014.[22] Blake emphasized his guitar playing on "Dissatisfied Blues," with its guitar-body knocks and mandolin-like solos, while he let his scat singing and horn imitations take center stage on "Miss Emma Liza." His performances on his follow-up 78, "Night and Day Blues" / "Sun to Sun," are among his least exciting. According to John Tefteller, owner of an outstanding collection of hard-to-find blues 78s, these two 78s are the rarest of all Blind Blake records, with only one copy of "Night and Day" / "Sun to Sun" known to exist.[23] The final Blind Blake release, recorded in June, is quite different from his other works. He strums his way through "Champagne Charlie Is My Name," an old Victorian music hall standard, and recasts the well-known "Sitting on Top of the World" melody in "Depression's Gone from Me Blues." On this final recording, Blake sounds is if he's using a flat pick for his string-bending solos.

What happened to Blind Blake after Paramount folded in 1932? For decades, the bluesman's final fate was uncertain. Then, in 2011, a death certificate for Arthur Blake was discovered by a team of researchers that included Alex van der Tuuk, Bob Eagle, Rob Ford, Eric LeBlanc, and Angela Mack. Their findings suggest that Blake spent the last two or three years of his life living at 1844 B North 10th Street in the Bronzeville section of Milwaukee, Wisconsin, with his wife Beatrice McGee Blake, whom he'd married around 1931. His death certificate listed his profession as "unemployed musician," and his date of death was entered as December 1, 1934, with pulmonary tuberculosis listed as the cause.[24]

For a while, Blind Blake's records sold almost as well as Blind Lemon Jefferson's, and he had a tremendous impact, especially in the Southeast. Personally, I'd like to believe Blind Blake lived the lines he sang in "Poker Woman Blues":

> *Sometime I'm rich, sometime I ain't got a cent,*
> *Sometime I'm rich, sometime I ain't got a cent,*
> *But I've had a good time everywhere I went.*[25]

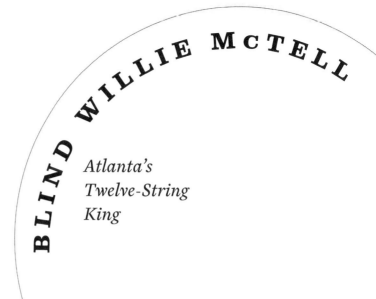

BLIND WILLIE McTELL

*Atlanta's
Twelve-String
King*

DURING THE ROARING TWENTIES, Atlanta, Georgia, was home to a thriving community of bluesmen whose styles were just as distinctive as those of their counterparts in Texas and Mississippi. Peg Leg Howell and His Gang specialized in countrified juke music set to guitar and violin. Barbecue Bob, who for a while was Columbia Records' best-selling bluesman, framed his songs with zesty bass runs and rhythmic slide played on a twelve-string guitar. His older brother Laughing Charley Lincoln was a less flashy twelve-stringer whose dark personality belied the "laughing" shtick on his 78s. Their childhood friend Curley Weaver expertly played six-string slide guitar as well as the old-time frailing and more recent "Piedmont" styles. Their associate Buddy Moss, a talented harmonica player and guitarist who came to prominence in the 1930s, drew from their sound, as well as what he had learned from records by Blind Blake and others. Blind Willie McTell, truly in a class of his own, emerged as one of the greatest bluesmen of any era.

Throughout his career, Blind Willie McTell favored Stella twelve-string guitars.
Courtesy Lawrence Cohn.

McTell had a shrewd mind, insightful lyrics, astounding nimble-
ness on a twelve-string guitar, and a sweet, plangent, slightly nasal
voice. Sensitive, confident, and hip-talking, he was a beloved figure
in the various communities in which he traveled. He played sub-
limely, a result both of natural talent and from performing hours a
day for people from all walks of life. McTell's records reveal a phe-
nomenal repertoire of blues, ragtime, hillbilly music, spirituals,
ballads, show tunes, and original songs. His records seldom sound
high-strung or harrowed, projecting instead an exuberant, upbeat
personality and indomitable spirit.

Blind since infancy, Willie Samuel McTier was most likely born in
1901.[1] During his 1940 Library of Congress session, McTell was asked
by John Lomax where he grew up. "I growed up down in south Georgia," McTell responded. "Statesboro, Georgia, was my *real* home. I was
born in Thomson, Georgia, 134 miles out of Atlanta, 37 miles west of
Augusta."[2] His mother was Minnie Watkins, and his father has been
variously identified as Eddie McTier and McTear. (Evidently Willie
adapted the phonetic "McTell" spelling taught to him in school.)
McTell fondly recalled his mother singing hymns and reading books
to him. During his Library of Congress session, he introduced his
performance of "Just As Well Get Ready, You Got to Die" by saying,
"I will demonstrate how my mother and father used to wander about
their work. When they used to sing those old-fashioned hymns. . . .
Then you'd see 'em wanderin' around the house, early in the mornin',
cookin' breakfast, tryin' to get ready to go to the fields, tryin' to
make some of the old country money. And way back in them days,
I hear one my own mother singed."[3] Relatives described Minnie
Watkins as an outstanding blues guitarist who began teaching her son

**Blind Willie McTell and his wife Kate, who supplied many important
details about his life history. Courtesy David Evans.**

six-string guitar when he was young. According to Willie's first wife, Kate McTell, he also played other instruments: "He could blow a harp. And I believe he played a banjo. A violin. [He was] very good, but he didn't like it. He just loved his guitar."[4]

When McTell was young, his father left the family. He moved with his mother to Statesboro, some seventy miles to the southeast and the center of a prosperous lumber and turpentine industry. For a while they lived in a shack near the railroad tracks, and then moved into a small house on Elm Street. An older blind girl down the street encouraged McTell to seek an education, which he did. A family friend, Josephus "Seph" Stapleton, showed him some guitar.[5] McTell's father, whom he visited from time to time, also played guitar. By his midteens, McTell was performing in traveling shows and on the streets of Statesboro. In 1917, his mother gave birth to his half brother, Robert Owens, for whom McTell always had a deep fondness. When their mother died in 1920, McTell returned to Thomson while Robert stayed with relatives in Statesboro. "After that I got on my own," McTell recalled. "I could go anywhere I want without telling anybody where I was."[6]

During his 1940 Library of Congress session, McTell told John Lomax that from 1922 through 1925 he attended the State Blind School in Macon.[7] There he learned to make brooms, work with clay and leather, and sew. (Later in life he'd make ashtrays, shoes, chairs, and pocketbooks.) He continued his education in private schools in New York and Michigan, learning to read Braille books and sheet music. He reportedly had perfect pitch, as his half brother Robert Owens claimed he could call out all the notes on a piano.

McTell became renowned for his unassailable sense of direction and extraordinary powers of perception and memory. He could hear the slightest whisper across a room, recognize hundreds of people by their voices, and navigate his way through city and countryside by using a tapping cane and a sort of personal sonar created by making a clucking sound with his tongue. Relatives described him as "earsighted." In her 1975 and 1976 interviews with the Evans family, published in *Blues Unlimited,* Kate McTell said,

> He felt like he could see in his world just like we could see in our world. And he could tell you how long hair was, what color I was. And if you walk up to him and spoke to him, he could tell you whether you were a black person or a white person. And he could tell you how tall you were, or whether you were short—just by listening to your voice. And he could tell you whether you were a heavyset person or a thin person. He was marvelous. He could go *anywhere* he wanted to go. He had a stick, and he'd go "Tch, tch, tch, tch," to the sound of that. He'd never bump or run into anything. He said that sound would go into whatever he was going close to, and so he would know to walk around it or to go around it.[8]

Photographs reveal that McTell favored twelve-string Stella guitars. Kate McTell recalled that he bought his instruments at a favorite store in Atlanta on Decatur Street near Five Points. "He'd trade them in and buy a new one," Kate told David Evans. "He always liked the [store]. They would always tune it up, you know, and everything, and he'd take it out and tune it himself. And he could hit the box and tell whether it was any good or not. And he always bought his guitars there. . . . If his guitar get to where he didn't want to play it anymore, he would take it and trade it in or put it away and buy him another one. He'd never have 'em repaired."[9]

He carried his guitar with him everywhere and treated it with great care. "He would never put his guitar in the back of nobody's car," Kate told Evans. "He'd always carry it on his back and hold it in his lap. He loved that guitar. He called it his baby."[10] One of his neighbors told researcher Peter B. Lowry that McTell had "a bunch of bottlenecks in his coat pocket" and used different ones for different songs.[11] McTell later began using a metal ring or thimble as well. He favored standard and open-G tunings and, unlike most of the Atlanta bluesmen, had a pronounced ragtime influence.

According to Kate McTell, her husband always bought his Stella twelve-strings at a music store on Decatur Street in Atlanta. Courtesy Stefan Grossman.

Blind Willie McTell inaugurated his recording career in October 1927, cutting a pair of 78s during the Victor label's field trip to Atlanta. After a pair of slideless blues, "Stole Rider Blues" and "Writing Paper Blues," McTell recorded the first of many slide masterpieces, "Mamma, Tain't Long Fo' Day," working his bass and treble strings in a manner that had more in common with Texas gospel great Blind Willie Johnson than Barbecue Bob and other Atlanta-based sliders. McTell signed a contract with Victor and a year later recorded two more 78s, including another masterwork, "Statesboro Blues." While this song is best known today as Duane Allman's signature bottleneck song with the Allman Brothers Band, the McTell version is slideless. (And credit where credit is due: Duane Allman did not invent the "Statesboro Blues" slide figures—these were created by Jesse Ed Davis on an earlier cover on Taj Mahal's 1967 debut album.)

All of McTell's initial Victor 78s were hardcore blues. In October 1929, he moonlighted for the first time with Columbia Records, which would release many of his more adventurous secular sides. McTell was in extraordinary form at his debut Columbia session, held in Atlanta. Among the four titles recorded on October 30 were two of his very best records, "Atlanta Strut" and "Travelin' Blues." In "Atlanta Strut" he sang of meeting up with a "gang of stags" and a little girl who

During "Travelin' Blues," one of the finest blues performances on record, McTell used his slider to mimic a train's engine, bell, and whistle. Courtesy Roger Misiewicz and Helge Thygesen.

looked "like a lump of lord have mercy," and then embarked upon a lyrical journey that warps and mutates like a Dali painting. Meanwhile, his booming twelve-string imitated a bass viol, cackling hen, crowing rooster, piano, slide guitar, even a man walking up the stairs! He fingerpicked "Travelin' Blues" with extraordinary finesse, using his slider to mimic a train's engine, bell, and whistle, and then doing a note-perfect quote of the familiar "Poor Boy" melody. Columbia identified him on records as "Blind Sammie," but for anyone who'd heard the Victor 78s, there was no mistaking this artist's identity. The following month, McTell recorded eight songs for Victor, but only two—"Drive Away Blues" / "Love Changing Blues"—were issued. McTell was back recording for Columbia in April 1930, and the label promoted "Talking to Myself" with a newspaper ad.

Columbia Records brought Blind Willie Johnson and his traveling companion, female singer Willie Harris, to Atlanta to record spiritual sides on April 20, 1930. Three days earlier, McTell had recorded "Talking to Myself" and "Razor Ball" at the same facility. Reference books have listed McTell as playing on the Blind Willie Johnson session as well, but the 78s themselves reveal that Johnson is the only guitarist. It is certain, though, that McTell and Johnson became friends and toured together. As McTell told John Lomax in 1940, "Blind Willie Johnson was a personal pal of mine. He and I played together on many different parts of the states and different parts of the country from Maine to Mobile Bay." McTell recalled that Johnson used a steel ring for slide and that the two of them enjoyed playing "I Got to Cross the River Jordan" together. When Lomax asked McTell if Johnson was a "good guitar picker," McTell responded, "Excellent good!"[12]

McTell's next flurry of sessions took place in October 1931. On the twenty-third, he cut the Columbia 78 "Southern Can Is Mine" / "Broke Down Engine Blues" and the OKeh 78 "Stomp Down Rider" / "Scarey Day Blues." He also backed Mary Willis on "Talkin' to You

Wimmen about the Blues" and three other songs. Curley Weaver, who'd become fast friends with McTell around 1930, accompanied him in the studio for the first time a week later. McTell played unsurpassed ragtime-influenced twelve-string on his unaccompanied "Georgia Rag," while the 78's flip side, "Low Rider's Blues," featured Weaver soloing with a bottleneck as McTell shouted encouragement. The duo also backed Willis on her OKeh releases "Low Down Blues" and "Merciful Blues." McTell's OKeh 78s were credited to "Georgia Bill."

As the Depression deepened, blues record sales plummeted. David Evans notes that in 1929, Columbia's initial pressings of McTell's "Travelin' Blues" / "Come on Around to My House Mama" numbered 2,205, followed by a second run of 2,000. When "Atlanta Strut" / "Kind Mama" finally came out in 1932, only 400 copies were pressed.[13] McTell's sole session of 1932 coupled him with another female singer, Ruby Glaze, for four songs. Bluebird identified him on the labels as "Blind Willie." The duo's 78 of "Lonesome Day Blues" sold only 124 copies and is among his rarest records today.[14] Meanwhile, sales of 78s by white musicians were much stronger: *78 Quarterly* estimated that McTell's Victor label mate Jimmie Rodgers's "Mississippi River Blues" sold 47,355 copies and the Carter Family's "On the Rock Where Moses Stood" sold 16,407.[15]

Despite the discouraging sales, McTell's luck at scoring record sessions held. In September 1933 he accompanied Curley Weaver and Buddy Moss to New York City for the marathon ARC session that, in hindsight, was the swansong of the early Atlanta blues guitar scene. McTell played second guitar on records credited to Curley Weaver and Buddy Moss, who in turn backed McTell on two dozen gospel and blues selections. As David Evans writes in his excellent liner notes for *The Definitive Blind Willie McTell,* "Weaver's work on second guitar, and occasionally second voice, is stunning throughout the sessions, whether he plays in slide style or fretting with the fingers. He is generally in a different key position or tuning from McTell and provides either a contrasting part or a more complex version of McTell's part that cuts through the fuller sound of the 12-string. These tracks represent some of the high points in blues duet recording, ranking with the best pieces by the Beale Street Sheiks, Tommy Johnson and Charlie McCoy, or Memphis Minnie and Kansas Joe."[16]

Vocalion Records credited McTell's 1933 recording of "Broke Down Engine" to "Blind Willie." He'd recorded an earlier version for Columbia. Courtesy Roger Misiewicz and Helge Thygesen.

McTell and Moss each recorded two versions of "Broke Down Engine" and covered Bumble Bee Slim's "B and O Blues" at the session, with Weaver accompanying each of them. Moss remembered that McTell acted as their leader in New York, both at the session and in navigating subways. The Moss and Weaver 78s came out on budget labels like Banner, Conqueror, Melotone, and Romeo. McTell's dozen issued sides were on the premium Vocalion label. His "Don't You See How This World Made a Change," with Weaver adding guitar and vocals, came out credited to "Blind Willie and Partner."[17]

While McTell kept a home base in Atlanta during the early 1930s, he rambled far and wide. During summers, he played for vacationers in Miami and the Georgia Sea Islands. When the tobacco crop came in July and August, he'd play at warehouses and hotels around Statesboro and further east in Winston-Salem and Durham, North Carolina. He refused to accept car rides from strangers and almost always journeyed by train, bus, or trolley. McTell was confident in his ability to support himself by playing for tips in train cars, stations and depots, small clubs, and on the street. He acted as his own manager and agent, arranging bookings by telephone. He had strong networks of friends and relatives, especially around Thomson and Statesboro, where he returned often and was universally known by his childhood nicknames of "Doog" and "Blind Doogie."

In Thomson, he enjoyed sitting under a relative's tree and playing for friends and passersby. On weekends he'd entertain at picnics, juke joints, and house parties. His Sunday mornings were typically spent playing guitar at the Jones Grove Baptist Church. In Statesboro, McTell enjoyed visiting his half brother Robert and a network of girlfriends, one of whom would chauffeur him around in an automobile he had bought her. Statesboro residents recalled him playing ragtime, blues, and pop songs for ladies' clubs, school assemblies, in front of hot dog stands and hotels, and in the homes of whites and blacks alike. He played spiritual music at a couple of local churches, sometimes accompanying gospel quartets. He collaborated with many musicians in the area, especially an outstanding slide guitar player named Lord Randolph Byrd, who was known locally as Blind Log and never recorded. The two traveled together to many Georgia towns and remained lifelong friends.

On January 10, 1934, Blind Willie McTell married Ruthy Kate Williams, a student he had heard singing at a high school ceremony in Augusta. McTell was drawn to her strong, countrified voice, and it turned out their mothers had been friends and had jokingly promised their young children to each other. Kate McTell said that as newlyweds she and Willie moved into an apartment at 381 Houston Street Northwest in Atlanta. Curley Weaver and his longtime girlfriend, Cora Thomson, also moved in, and the two couples lived there for several years. Kate joined the choir at the Big Bethel A.M.E. Church, and her husband paid for her to attend college and earn a nursing degree.[18]

While Kate was in school, Willie was often on the road. "I said to Willie once, I said, 'Willie,' I said, 'you got me stuck here in nursing school and you stay gone all the time.' He said, 'Baby, I was born a rambler. I'm gonna ramble until I die,' he said, 'but I'm preparing you to live after I'm gone.' He did. He sure did."[19] On occasion, Kate helped Willie with his songwriting. "He'd just think 'em up. And he'd come home and maybe give me a line or two to write. And then he'd say, 'What did I tell you to write last night?' I said, 'Such and such a thing.' He says, 'Oh, well, this'll be another one. Turn over to another page and write this down.' The way he composed would be, write down words. Then we would sing 'em and see how they sound with the guitar. Sometimes he'd change 'em around."[20] She also remembered that he would spontaneously create blues songs as he played.

On occasion, Kate sang spirituals with her husband and danced onstage when he played matinees at the 81 Theatre, sometimes with

Victor sales records reveal that a total of 4,010 copies of Blind Willie McTell's debut 78, "Stole Rider Blues" / "Mr. McTell Got the Blues," were sold. Courtesy Roger Misiewicz and Helge Thygesen.

Curley Weaver sitting in. After seeing one such performance there in 1935, recording executive Mayo Williams invited the McTells and Weaver to Chicago to record for Decca Records. At these Chicago sessions, the McTells performed several old-time gospel slide tunes reminiscent of Blind Willie Johnson with Willie Harris. Weaver joined McTell on "Bell Street Blues," "Cold Winter Day," and "Cooling Board Blues," finessing quick-fingered solos behind McTell's twelve-string bass parts and rhythm. McTell backed Weaver on a half-dozen blues as well, including a rare appearance on six-string guitar on two of Weaver's best records, "Oh Lawdy Mama" and "Tricks Ain't Walking No More." McTell was paid a hundred dollars per side—excellent pay during the Depression—although few of these records were issued at the time.

None of the records from his next session, held by Vocalion in Augusta in July 1936 with Piano Red, were issued. According to Kate, "They said he sang and played too loud. You know, he had a *real* loud voice. He thought he [Piano Red] was too high for his type of music. You see, Willie played a guitar, and the piano would drown the guitar out."[21]

For two summers, the McTells toured with a medicine show that featured a pair of blackface comedians and a barker who sold "rattlesnake liniment." Kate's role, she explained to Cheryl Thurber, was to dance while her husband played: "I Charlestoned and Black Bottomed, the old Charleston and Black Bottom, and tap dance. We showed in Louisville, Kentucky. And we did a lot through Georgia too, during the summer months when I wasn't in school."[22] The troupe traveled by bus, train, and car, and McTell was paid a salary. Occasionally they set up a tent, but most of the time they performed outdoors in courthouse squares. Around 1938, the McTells traveled to California and visited Oakland for a week. When Kate's school was in session, McTell would often travel with his friend Curley Weaver. "Willie did most of the leading, and he was always the manager," Kate explained. "He would always book the recordings or wherever they would play at, you know. And they would pay it to Willie, and then Willie would pay Curley."[23]

Eventually, the McTells moved to an apartment on Atlanta's northeast side, near downtown. Kate recalled that Willie was particularly fond of collard greens, potatoes, and potato pie. They had a living room, kitchen, bedroom, and a music room where he stored

McTell poses in a photographer's studio with his favorite guitar and a white cane.
Courtesy David Evans.

his instruments. McTell especially enjoyed his music room, where he read Braille books from the library, took naps on his couch before going out to work, and enjoyed a hot toddy before bed. He often played at Yates' Drug Store on the corner of Butler and Auburn during the day, and spent evenings serenading customers in parked cars at the Pig 'n' Whistle, a drive-in barbecue restaurant on Ponce de Leon Avenue.[24] Here, McTell likely covered a wide variety of popular songs. As Peter B. Lowry wrote, "I firmly believe that if you happened upon Willie on Ponce de Leon, gave him a quarter, and requested 'Beer Barrel Polka,' you'd get it. He was a blind, professional musician—this is how he made his living."[25]

Kate explained to Cheryl Thurber, "Different cars would call for him, you know. Well, this car would say, 'I got him.' And another car would say, 'I want the musician over here,' you know. And they say, 'Well, I got him for an hour,' or so long. And they would just pay him for that length of time. And then another car would call for him. [He was paid by] peoples in the cars. The Pig 'n' Whistle paid him too. He would take requests, but he was just continually playing unless they requested certain songs for him to play."[26] On Saturdays, the McTells would perform sets at the 81 Theatre from 4:00 until 9:00, and then Willie would head over to the Pig 'n' Whistle. On Sundays, the McTells occasionally performed at the Mt. Zion Baptist Church.

In one of the more fortuitous meetings in blues history, folklorist John Lomax and his wife found McTell serenading at the Pig 'n' Whistle in November 1940 and brought him to their hotel to record for the Library of Congress's Archive of American Folk Song. On the journey to the hotel McTell called out directions and pointed to landmarks as if he could see them. This noncommercial session yielded a breathtaking array of folk ballads, spirituals, blues, and ragtime songs, and insightful monologues on old songs, blues history, and life itself. McTell's lively cover of "Dying Crapshooter's Blues," a poetic and ambitious composition that had previously been recorded by vaudeville singers, showcased an unforgettable melody. "Delia," later recorded by Johnny Cash, came out of the nineteenth-century ballad tradition.

McTell's lonesome slide during the spirituals "I Got to Cross the River Jordan," "Old Time Religion," and "Amazing Grace" recalled Blind Willie Johnson's 78s, especially in the way he'd use his slider to produce a string of notes and harmonic overtones from a single strike of the string. Lomax was aware of this connection, introducing "I Got to Cross the River Jordan" by saying, "This is a song played by Blind Willie McTell, which he says he used to sing and play with Blind Willie Johnson." McTell quickly added, "This is a song that I'm gonna play that we all used to play in the country—an old jubilee melody."[27] Like Johnson, McTell played his version in open tuning. He prefaced "Amazing Grace" by describing how it was played on banjo in the old-time churches of his youth. When he finished his instrumental performance, he said, "Now, that's a song that our

Blind Willie McTell recording in an Atlanta hotel room for the Library of Congress, November 5, 1940. Photograph by John Lomax, Library of Congress.

mothers and fathers used to hum back in the days when they'd be pickin' cotton, pullin' corn—farmer's work."[28]

In less than an hour, McTell gave the American public some of the finest records he'd ever make. But the Library of Congress session did not go easily for McTell. One of the more telling exchanges between the folklorist and the bluesman occurred when Lomax asked McTell if he knew "any songs about colored people havin' hard times here in the South. . . . Complainin' about the hard times and sometimes mistreatment of the whites. Have you got any songs that talk about that?" "No, sir," McTell responded. "I haven't, not at the present time, because the whites is mighty good to the Southern people, as far as I know." Lomax pressed on: "'Ain't It Hard to Be a Nigger, Nigger'—do you know that one?" "No," McTell answered. "That's not our time." A moment later Lomax observed, "You keep movin' around like you're uncomfortable. What's the matter, Willie?" McTell quickly shifted to another topic: "Well, I was in an automobile accident last night, little shook up. No one got hurt, but it was all jostled up mighty bad. Shake up—still sore from it, but no one got hurt."[29]

Not long after America entered World War II, Willie and Kate McTell separated. She moved to Augusta and became a civil service nurse, while Willie stayed in Atlanta and eventually began living with Helen Edwards, who took the name Helen McTell and stayed with Willie until her death in 1958. During the 1940s McTell began receiving assistance checks for his blindness and, without any record deals, mainly played house parties and at the Pig 'n' Whistle. He continued to visit relatives in Statesboro, where he'd play at the Silver Moon, and Augusta, where Good Time Charlie's tavern was a favorite venue.

The jump blues of T-Bone Walker and other electric bluesmen became a dominant sound on jukeboxes and in radio broadcasts just after World War II. But by the late 1940s, the more visceral, stripped-down records of John Lee Hooker, Muddy Waters, and Lightnin' Hopkins were beginning to attract an audience. In May 1949, an executive from the New Jersey-based Regal Records advertised on an Atlanta radio station for country-blues guitarists. Blind Willie McTell and Curley Weaver answered the call, cutting twenty blues and gospel selections at a studio on Edgewood Avenue. These excellent-sounding records reveal a wealth of innovative bass lines, interesting chords, masterfully fingerpicked solos, and sublime slide, especially on the songs McTell fronted. Their exciting "You Can't Get That Stuff No More" revisited a 1932 Tampa Red hit, and McTell's remakes of "Love Changin' Blues" and "Savannah Women" featured sweet and low-down slide. "Pal of Mine" was a Tin Pan Alley pop song McTell had sung with medicine shows. Weaver, who played a six-string at the session, recorded three selections with McTell's support, singing with a strong voice on "Wee Midnight Hours," "Brown Skin Woman," and "I Keep on Drinkin'." From this session, Regal issued only a few songs, although today they're all available on the Biograph CD *Pig 'n' Whistle Red*. On the issued 78s, "Hide Me in Thy Bosom" and "It's My Desire" were credited to "Blind Willie," and one of the blues songs identified him as "Pig 'n' Whistle Red."[30]

Blind Willie McTell's next sessions took place during autumn 1949. Ahmet Ertegun saw him playing alone on a street corner and convinced him to make recordings for his fledgling Atlantic Records. "I had collected many recordings he had made for RCA Victor, and I thought I recognized his voice, but I wasn't sure," Ertegun wrote to filmmaker David Fulmer in 1991. "I asked him his name and discovered he was 'the' famous Blind Willie McTell. He spoke of having no interest in recording anything except religious music, and would only play the blues if I would release it under another name. Therefore, we decided on the pseudonym Barrelhouse Sammy. He was a charming, ebullient, but soft-mannered person."[31]

For these Atlantic sessions, McTell reprised songs he'd recorded for Lomax—"Kill It Kid," "Delia," "Dying Crapshooter's Blues"—as well as blues, a rag, and several spirituals played slide-style. With its thunderous bass runs and behind-the-bridge strums, McTell's cover of "Pinetop's Boogie Woogie" almost sounded like prescient rock and roll. On subsequent listening to the acetates, though, Atlantic executives apparently deemed McTell's solitary blues a thing of the past, and his sole Atlantic single, "Kill It Kid" backed with "Broke Down Engine Blues," came out credited to "Barrelhouse Sammy (The Country Boy)." During the 1970s, most of the session was issued on the excellent Atlantic album *Atlanta Twelve String*. The high-fidelity sound of these recordings is quite extraordinary. Steve Hoffman, renowned for his work remastering classic albums, explains how McTell was likely recorded: "I asked Tom Dowd about it, and he knew how it was done. He told me they used a portable Magnecord PT-6 full-track octal machine and a single RCA ribbon mike, a 77DX, and Scotch 112 tape. Sometimes the simple things in life are best."[32]

In 1950 McTell and Helen Edwards moved to 1003 Dimmock Street, the last residence he'd have in Atlanta. McTell began frequenting the Blue Lantern Club, an all-white restaurant on Ponce de Leon Avenue, performing tableside as well as in the parking lot. He sang tenor for the Glee Club of the Metropolitan Atlanta Association for the Blind and played religious music on radio broadcasts from stations in Atlanta and Decatur. Around 1952 he acquired an electric guitar, but according to Kate, whom he'd visit once or twice a year, "he just liked his 12-string better, and he quit it. He went back to the 12-string."[33]

Overweight, drinking heavily, suffering from diabetes, and occasionally losing his balance, McTell seldom traveled beyond Atlanta, Thomson, and Statesboro in the mid-1950s, and he required hospital care from time to time. In September 1956, McTell made his final

Blind Willie McTell, circa 1950, when he lived on Dimmock Street in Atlanta. Courtesy David Evans.

recordings for Ed Rhodes, who owned a record store on Peachtree Street near the Blue Lantern Club. McTell was supplied with corn liquor, and while he seemed to get looser as the session progressed, he nonetheless played with drive and precision. McTell played all eighteen selections without a slide, covering songs from his early days, his Library of Congress session, and his postwar sessions with Curley Weaver. He also covered pop songs, old blues by Blind Blake and the Hokum Boys, and hillbilly numbers such as "Wabash Cannonball," telling Rhodes, "I jump 'em from other writers, but I arrange 'em my way."

McTell quit playing blues soon afterward, when he got the calling to preach. He became a deacon at the Mt. Zion Baptist Church, using a Braille bible and dedicating himself to helping blind people. His health declined rapidly after his companion Helen died in November 1958, and in the spring of 1959 he suffered a stroke that caused partial paralysis. McTell's cousin Eddie McTear moved him back to Thomson. That summer he suffered another stroke and was taken to the Milledgeville State Hospital, where he died from a cerebral hemorrhage on August 19, 1959. Among the items in his estate were an acoustic six-string guitar, three acoustic twelve-strings, and an electric guitar and amplifier. McTell's wish to be buried with one of his twelve-string guitars was not honored, and due to a stone-carver's error, his original tombstone bore the name of his relative who had commissioned the engraving:

Eddie McTier
1898
AUG 19 1959
At Rest[34]

Thirty years later, a proper gravestone and roadside historical marker were placed near Blind Willie McTell's grave in the Jones Grove Baptist Church cemetery, seven miles south of Thomson. In

1983, Bob Dylan paid him tribute in his memorable ballad "Blind Willie McTell," singing, "Nobody can sing the blues like Blind Willie McTell." A decade later, Dylan covered McTell's "Broke Down Engine" and "Delia" on *World Gone Wrong*.

While Blind Willie McTell and his contemporaries in Atlanta (Barbecue Bob, Curley Weaver, Peg Leg Howell) created hundreds of excellent blues recordings, precious little of their influence resounds in modern music. Unlike their contemporaries in Chicago and Mississippi, their sound did not become a cornerstone of postwar blues and rock and roll, but rather a glimpse back at a bygone era. Fortunately, virtually everything they recorded is now available, and much of it sounds just as poignant as when first recorded.

In this Columbia publicity shot, sublime gospel-blues guitarist Blind Willie Johnson holds a small-bodied acoustic guitar. Courtesy John Tefteller.

BLIND WILLIE JOHNSON

Sublime
Gospel Blues

A SINGING STREET-CORNER EVANGELIST, Blind Willie Johnson created some of the most intensely moving records of the twentieth century. Void of frivolity or uncertainty, his 78s are clearly the work of a pained believer seeking redemption. A slide guitarist nonpareil, Johnson had an exquisite sense of timing and tone, using a pocket-knife or ring slider to duplicate his vocal inflections or to produce an unforgettable phrase from a single strike of a string. Eric Clapton credits his "It's Nobody's Fault but Mine" as "probably the finest slide guitar playing you'll ever hear."[1] Jack White cites Johnson's "Dark Was the Night—Cold Was the Ground" as "the greatest example of slide guitar ever recorded,"[2] while Ry Cooder calls the track "the most transcendent piece in all American music."

"Blind Willie Johnson had great dexterity," Cooder describes, "because he could play all of these sparking little melody lines. He had fabulous syncopation; he could keep his thumb going really strong. He's so good—I mean, he's just *so good!* Beyond being a guitar player, I think the guy is one of these interplanetary world musicians, the kind of person they talk about in that Nada Brahma book, where the world is sound and everything is resonating. He's one of those guys. There's only a few. Blind Willie Johnson is in the ether somewhere. He's up there in the zone."[3]

There's a thin, sometimes indistinguishable line between Blind Willie Johnson's spiritual songs and old-time country blues, and it's no surprise that many blues musicians adapted songs he popularized. Son House, for instance, recorded sublime a capella versions of "Motherless Children" and "John the Revelator." Accompanied by the Hunter's Chapel Singers, Mississippi Fred McDowell recorded a stellar version of "Keep Your Lamp Trimmed and Burning." Reverend Gary Davis recast "If I Had My Way" as "Samson and Delilah." Texas bluesman Mance Lipscomb delighted listeners with his pocketknife-slide versions of "God Moves on the Water," "Nobody's Fault but Mine," and "Motherless Children," which he said he learned from Johnson himself. Long after his death, Blind Willie Johnson entered into the rock and modern blues mainstreams through covers by Led Zeppelin, the Grateful Dead, Blues Project, Ten Years After, Jorma Kaukonen, Eric Clapton, Ben Harper, Bruce Springsteen, the White Stripes, and many others.

As inspiring a player as Blind Willie Johnson was, few historic documents link directly to him. The most revealing is his death certificate, filed on September 21, 1945, in Beaumont, Texas. The name "Angilina Johnson" appears in the document's signature section, so presumably his widow, Angeline, provided the information. According to this document, Willie Johnson Jr. was born on January 22, 1897, in Independence, Texas. His parents are listed as Willie Johnson Sr. of Mississippi and Mary Fields of Moody, Texas. The document further shows that Johnson had lived at 1440 Forest Street in Beaumont for "30 years" and worked as a minister.[4]

A second document, a 1918 draft registration card, may also relate to Blind Willie Johnson. The strongest details linking it to the musician are the date of birth—January 25, 1897—and the fact that it states that this Willie Johnson, aged twenty-one, had been blind for "13 years," which tallies with a statement Angeline made that her husband was blinded at age seven. But the father listed on the draft card is "Dock Johnson," and Pendleton, Texas, is given as his place of birth.[5] "Willie Johnson," obviously, is a common name, and it is possible that this draft card relates to another person.

In his seminal 1959 book *The Country Blues,* Samuel Charters, who found and interviewed Angeline Johnson in 1953, provides yet another scenario for Johnson's early life: "Blind Willie was born on a farm outside of Marlin, Texas, a small town east of the Brazos River. His father was named George Johnson. When Willie was three or four years old, about 1905, his mother died and his father married again. About the time he was seven years old, his father caught his second wife with another man and beat her. To get even with Willie's father she threw a pan of lye water in the little boy's face, blinding him."[6]

Blind Willie Johnson spent most of his youth in Marlin, a bustling town at the time. The city was renowned for its curative hot mineral waters, bath houses, sanitariums, sumptuous hotels, and clement weather. A pre-1930s promotional brochure praised the city's "twelve modern churches," "modern electric light, power, and ice plant," "fifty-four miles of graded, graveled, and well-drained residence streets," and its "pressed brick plant, modern steam laundry, planning mill, compress, oil mill, three cotton gins, numerous garages, vulcanizing plants and supply houses."[7] The New York Giants baseball team headquartered its off-season training camp in Marlin.

Young Johnson attended the Church of God in Christ on Commerce Street. The denomination encouraged energetic music making, and by age five, Johnson had told his father that he wanted to be a "beecher," as he mispronounced "preacher."[8] His father crafted his first guitar from a cigar box. In time, Johnson became skilled in both standard tuning and the open-D tuning he used for slide. Many of his songs were culled from old hymnals, such as the 1881 copy of T. C. O'Kane's *Redeemer's Praise for the Sunday-School, Church, and Family* that Angeline gave Sam Charters. "Willie sang in the churches and for religious meetings on the outskirts of town," Charters reported. "In the winter months he would stand in the wind, playing an incessant, rasping guitar accompaniment to his rough voice, until his fingers were stiff with the cold. A tin cup was fashioned with wire to the neck of his guitar so people could drop coins in while he was playing."[9] Some of Marlin's older residents remembered that Johnson was influenced by a local blind preacher and singer named Madkin Butler, who taught him at least one of the songs he'd record, "Everybody Ought to Treat a Stranger Right."[10] Madkin apparently didn't play any instruments, and Johnson was occasionally seen accompanying him at Baptist church gatherings.

Elder residents of Hearne, Texas, recalled Johnson singing on the streets in the mid-1920s. "His father was farming outside of town," Charters wrote. "He would bring Willie in from the farm and Willie would sit under an awning singing as the crowds of people, in from the farms to shop, would walk past. Toward the end of the afternoon, the shopping done, they would stand listening. Hearne was a brickyard town, with nine yards working. There was money for street beggars and singers."[11] Blind Lemon Jefferson would also frequent Hearne, and residents remembered Johnson singing gospel on one street corner while Blind Lemon Jefferson sang blues on another. Both men had stentorian voices, rhythmic drive, and a special facility with staccato, by-the-bridge bass runs, so it's possible they may have exchanged information. Jefferson, however, recorded very little on slide guitar—just two 1926 takes of "Jack O' Diamond Blues"—while Johnson did his very best work with a slide.

Around 1926 Johnson married Willie Harris, who had seen him playing guitar and piano at church services and revival meetings. During their marriage they resided in a small house at 817 Hunter

Street in Marlin. Willie Harris, who had a beautiful, countrified voice, would accompany Blind Willie Johnson on several of his 1928 and 1930 recordings. In 1931 the couple had a child, Sam Faye Johnson. Her birth certificate lists her father as "Willie Johnson, musician," and her mother's maiden name is "Willie B. Hays." In a 2003 interview with Michael Corcoran, Sam Faye Johnson Kelly shared her memory of her father: "I remember him sitting here in the kitchen and reciting from the Bible. But I was just a little girl when he went away." During this period, Kelly recalled, her mother worked "seven days a week as a nurse."[12]

Which brings us to another mystery regarding the life of Blind Willie Johnson: when did he marry Angeline? Her account of their first meeting, in Dallas, was included in the liner notes for Yazoo Records' *Praise God I'm Satisfied* album:

> He was singin' on the street, an' he was singin' "If I Had-a My Way," an' I went walkin' behind him. I asked him, I says, "Say, are you married or single?" He says: "I'm, uh, single." An' I say: "Come go to my house; I have a piano," an' I say: "an' we will get together and sing." And he says: "Have you ever singed anywhere?" I said: "I sing over the radio and at our church." An' so he says: "All right." We went over to the house an' we sit down an' taken a few drinks, you know, an' played; then he played his guitar an' I got up to the piano an' I went to playin' "If I Had-a My Way"; he says, "Go on, gal!" He say: "Tear it up!" We went on back. He says: "Well, let's get on the street." I say, "Well, look! Don't you want something to eat?" He says: "What have you to cook?" I says: "Well, I have some crabs." I say: "We're makin' the old-time niggers' gumbo!" I say: "Don't you want some??!!" An' he says, "Well, yes." He says: "Say! Uh, let's marry!" An' I says "Okay," that's what I wanted. He says: "Well, when can you get ready?" I say: "I'll get ready tomorrow."

They reportedly married the following day, June 22.[13] In Charters's *The Country Blues* and other sources, the year of this marriage has been given as 1927, but no marriage certificate has been found to confirm this.

According to Willie Harris, her marriage to Johnson ended around 1932 or 1933. "It is possible that Willie was with both women over the same period of years," Charters speculated in his liner notes to Columbia/Legacy's *The Complete Blind Willie Johnson,* "but the relationship with Angeline could easily have begun around the time his marriage to the other woman was ending."[14] Further muddying these waters is a statement by Angeline that she stayed home in Beaumont with their child while Blind Willie Johnson was off making records. "They come and get him and carried him," she told Charters. "He'd be gone sometime thirty days, something like that, but he wouldn't be over there doing all that much work. He would, you know, just go, and then after he'd go, he'd just stay over there and then play on the streets. He loved to play on the streets."[15]

In December 1927, the Columbia record company sent Frank Walker to Dallas to make field recordings of African American musicians. It was the label's first foray into Texas, and over the course of five days Walker and his team would capture a wide array of musical styles. On December 2, they produced two 78s by blues singer Lillian Glinn backed by pianist Willie Tyson, followed by two 78s by Washington Phillips, who accompanied his gospel songs on a keyboard-operated fretless zither. His haunting and beautiful "Take Your Burden to the Lord" is a must-hear. The following day, the Columbia unit kicked off the day with Billiken Johnson and Fred Adams; Billiken Johnson's shtick was using his voice to create sound effects such as a train whistle and braying mule. Next up was the Dallas String Band's Coley Jones, making his recording debut as a solo singer/guitarist, and pianist Willie Tyson, recording the only 78 issued under his own name.[16]

Then it was Blind Willie Johnson's turn. He jump-started what was to be one of the greatest single-day sessions of the prewar blues and gospel era with a slide masterpiece, "I Know His Blood Can Make Me Whole." He then cut his enduring renditions of "Jesus

Make Up My Dying Bed" and "It's Nobody's Fault but Mine," and sang of a pain he knew all too well in "Mother's Children Have a Hard Time," one of the saddest songs imaginable. (Columbia got the title wrong on its initial release; on rerelease, the song was correctly titled "Motherless Children.") Johnson followed with his landmark instrumental "Dark Was the Night—Cold Was the Ground." He then retuned his guitar to standard for "If I Had My Way I'd Tear the Building Down," a slideless retelling of the Samson and Delilah story. On December 6, Columbia's field unit wrapped up their visit with the full Dallas String Band's debut recordings, harmonica wizard William McCoy's tour de force "Train Imitations and the Fox Chase," and the only 78s issued by singers Hattie Hudson and Gertrude Perkins.[17]

Columbia Records' 1929 advertisement invited record buyers to "Hear Blind Willie Johnson spread the light of old-time faith." Courtesy of the author.

Among these artists, Blind Willie Johnson would become the most popular. His records were unlike anything previously released by Columbia—or any other label, for that matter. The original advertisement for his first 78—"I Know His Blood Can Make Me Whole" backed with "Jesus Make Up My Dying Bed"—proclaimed: "This new and exclusive Columbia artist sings sacred songs in a way you have never heard before. Be sure to hear his first record and listen close to that guitar accompaniment. Nothing like it anywhere else."[18] The company had faith in the release, doing an initial pressing of 9,400 copies, priced at seventy-five cents apiece. Sales were strong. Their second run produced another 6,000 copies.[19] Blind Willie Johnson was soon one of Columbia's best-selling race artists, and his influence on other artists, especially Southern gospel singers, was immediate and long-lasting. During the next few years, four of his 78s were popular enough to be issued on both the Columbia and Vocalion labels.

Upon its release, the second Blind Willie Johnson 78, "It's Nobody's Fault But Mine" backed with "Dark Was the Night—Cold Was the Ground," was reviewed by Edward Abbe Niles in a national magazine, *Bookman.* Niles singled out Johnson's "violent, tortured and abysmal shouts and groans and his inspired guitar playing in a primitive and frightening Negro religious song."[20] A meditation cast in hums, moans, and ghostly slide, "Dark Was the Night—Cold Was the Ground" was a reworking of a well-known hymn about Jesus Christ's crucifixion. The hymn's full title helps clarify its meaning: "Dark Was the Night and Cold Was the Ground on Which Our Lord Was Laid." Ry Cooder recast Johnson's instrumental arrangement as the centerpiece of his *Paris, Texas* soundtrack. "I've tried all my life—worked very hard and every day of my life, practically—to play in that style," Cooder says. "Not consciously saying, 'Today's Tuesday; I will again try to play like Blind Willie Johnson,' you know, but that sound is in my head. The single-string melody thing that he did is so great, and he's just so good. And 'Dark Was the Night' is *the* cut. You can throw that lick at anybody nowadays—everybody relates. It's like an unspoken word."[21]

How did Johnson achieve his distinctive guitar sound? In his sole surviving photograph, a Columbia publicity shot, he holds a small twelve-fret acoustic, possibly a Stella, Harmony, or pre-Kay Stromberg-Voisinet. This may have been the guitar used at the

Johnson's monumental recording of "Dark Was the Night—Cold Was the Ground" still travels through space aboard the *Voyager 1* spacecraft. Courtesy Roger Misiewicz and Helge Thygesen.

session or just a photographer's prop. One of the keys to Johnson's tone, Cooder speculates, is how he held his slider:

> I've seen this blind preacher from Mississippi, Reverend Leon Pinson, play holding a bar between his left-hand finger and thumb. He reaches around underneath—like you normally would—and gets a very similar vibrato to Blind Willie Johnson's. It has that quality of coming up to the note and never quite hitting it. That's a very inexact technique, but it does give you the quarter-tones and all of the strange nuances. Blind Willie Johnson had great dexterity and fabulous syncopation; he could keep his thumb going real strong. He had the best left-hand vibrato— the absolute best. Very light touch, real light, and really fast. But that vibrato, I think you can only do it by wiggling that bar just right.[22]

Columbia's field unit returned to Dallas in December 1928 to record sixteen musical acts ranging from Frenchy's String Band, Rev. J. W. Heads, and the Texas Jubilee Singers to the returning Washington Phillips, Billiken Johnson, Dallas String Band, and Blind Willie Johnson. Cutting four songs on December 5, Johnson was accompanied by the plaintive vocal harmonies of Willie Harris. Johnson began his session with "I'm Gonna Run to the City of Refuge," using a straightforward strumming playing approach similar to "If I Had My Way I'd Tear the Building Down." In the harrowing "Jesus Is Coming Soon," also played without a slide, he sang of the catastrophic 1918 Spanish influenza epidemic, warning people to "turn away from evil and seek the Lord and pray." His third song, the slide tune "Lord I Just Can't Keep from Crying," inspired many covers both spiritual and secular, as did his final and arguably best selection of the day, "Keep Your Lamp Trimmed and Burning." In addition to the stellar vocal interplay between Johnson and Harris, this song showcases his brilliant technique of playing slide solos in the middle and upper ranges of the guitar. I once mentioned these 1928 recordings to Country Joe McDonald, who responded, "Blind Willie Johnson with his wife was just unbelievable. You're hearing a flash from the past, the tradition alive. Her singing has a modal plaintiveness that's a line going back to West Africa and to Portugal and to the Muslim prayer chanting. It's so spooky."[23]

Blind Willie Johnson's next session took place on December 10, 1929, in New Orleans. He performed four songs alone that day. Played in standard tuning, his congregation-rousing "Let Your Light Shine on Me" had been published in the early 1920s by evangelist Homer Rodeheaver. Johnson's version jumped tempos, moving from slow chordal rhythms to chugging strumming to flashy bass runs. Johnson reentered the slide zone in "God Don't Never Change," once again singing of the influenza epidemic. He also played slide on one of his gentlest, most laid-back recordings, "Bye and Bye I'm Goin' to See the King." He retuned to standard and resurrected his gruff voice for a lackluster, slightly out-of-tune version of the white gospel hymn "Sweeter as the Years Go By." As Samuel Charters wrote of the song, "For once the guitar accompaniment sounded clumsy and ordinary. He seemed to be running out of material, as happened to all but a handful of country singers, and he drifted into a style of song and playing that was badly suited to his own way of performing."[24]

Johnson hit his stride the following day, when he was accompanied by a female singer—possibly Willie B. Richardson—on five of his six selections. They began with the passionate slide tune "You'll Need Somebody on Your Bond," which Johnson would recut with Willie Harris at his final session four months later. Johnson tuned to standard and set aside his slider for the next four songs. The bright-toned bass figures in "When the War Was On," "Praise God I'm Satisfied," "Take Your Burden to the Lord and Leave It There," and "Take a Stand" fit the Texas country-blues tradition of Blind Lemon Jefferson and suggest that Johnson may have used a pick at the session. For his final song, Johnson retuned to open D and delivered one of his very best slide performances—"God Moves on the Water," an exhilarating account of the *Titanic* tragedy. "I love 'God Moves on the Water' so much," Cooder says. "That thing is like a roller coaster. He's got an energy wave in there that he's surfing across the face of that tune so mighty. He hits a chorus, and it's just like ice skating or downhill racing. It's an awesome physical thing that happens."[25]

Willie Harris was on hand—and in fine form—at Blind Willie Johnson's final session, held in Atlanta on Sunday, April 20, 1930. In all, the duo recorded ten songs. The engineer moved Harris close to the microphone, and her sweet vocals imparted a lulling effect to the music. Singing call-and-response and harmony vocals in a gentle voice, Johnson effectively used his slide in "Can't Nobody Hide from God," which gave Harris as prominent a vocal role as his. Harris sang the lead vocals on their version of the old white hymn "If It Had Not Been for Jesus." As Charters aptly wrote of the tune, "Its sentimentality and melodic triteness was poorly suited to Johnson's style. It's in 3/4 time, with simple chords, and his playing was limited to ordinary accompaniment. She sang the verses, and they sang in unison on the choruses. Her voice was sweet and direct, but nothing could help the song."[26] The pair followed the same pattern on the strangely titled "Go with Me to That Land," which fans of 1960s folk music will recognize as "Come and Go with Me."

Johnson and Harris picked up the pace for "The Rain Don't Fall on Me," "Trouble Will Soon Be Over," "The Soul of a Man," and "Everybody Ought to Treat a Stranger Right." Still playing slideless in standard tuning, Johnson balanced chord strums and bass runs on these selections. Next came a rousing rendition of "Church I'm Fully Saved Today." As Charters pointed out, "The form is a call and response, and he played an alternate chord strum that had some of the free swing of a jazz group. It isn't difficult to close your eyes and hear the song with tambourines and more guitars—the entire congregation joined in on the responses, feet stamping on the floor and hands clapping. With only two voices and his guitar they caught the whole mood of Southern evangelism."[27] Johnson and Harris followed with another classic, "John the Revelator." Johnson retuned to open D and used a slide on the final song, "You're Gonna Need Somebody on Your Bond," which surpasses the version he had recorded months earlier in New Orleans.

By 1930, the Depression was in full swing, and Columbia saw a precipitous drop in their record sales. Blind Willie Johnson, though, continued to outsell Bessie Smith and most of the label's country-blues artists. Robert Dixon and John Godrich reported in *Recording the Blues,*

> Blind Willie Johnson's first records had sold no better than the average disc in the Columbia 14000D series—in early 1929 they would manage about 5,000 as against Barbecue Bob's 6,000 and Bessie Smith's 9,000 or 10,000. But in mid-1930 the blind evangelist became the star of the list—his records were still selling 5,000 copies, although Barbe-cue Bob was down to 2,000, Bessie Smith to 3,000, and the average release had an initial sales of only just over 1,000. Columbia issued seven records by Blind Willie in 1930, but, as times became harder the following year, even his appeal waned. In 1931, like Barbecue Bob, Bessie Smith and the rest, Blind Willie's records were selling in the hundreds rather than thousands.[28]

As the Depression deepened, only nine hundred copies were pressed of the final Blind Willie Johnson 78 issued by Columbia, "Sweeter as the Years Go By" / "Take Your Stand," which came

Columbia Records told the truth when promoting Blind Willie Johnson's debut 78: "Nothing like it anywhere else." Courtesy of the author.

out in October 1931. Blind Willie Johnson never recorded again for a major label. Angeline told Charters of their recording songs together at a small studio in Beaumont, but no record is known to have survived this session.

After his final Columbia session, Blind Willie Johnson returned to Beaumont, Texas, where he'd live the rest of his life. Located along the Gulf of Mexico, Beaumont had been a major oil producer since the turn of the century. During the 1930s, the Works Progress Administration (WPA) ordered members of its Writers' Program to prepare a report on Beaumont, which in 1930 had a population of 57,700. "The influx of Negro labor for the refineries, shipyards and wharves and for domestic services has increased this part of the population to nearly one-third of the total," the WPA reported. "The city has a considerable Negro section with a motion picture theater, offices, churches, schools, stores, and many attractive homes. This section has its own lawyers, ministers, dentists, doctors, and teachers. Among its residents, however, there are those who practice 'charms,' whose lives are ruled by superstition, and whose picturesque manner of speech has crept into the current idiom."[29]

In Beaumont, Johnson sang at Mount Olive Baptist Church, sometimes accompanying the Silver Fleece Quartet and other younger singers. He also played along Forsythe Street, which ran through the heart of the city. In his later years, Charters described, Johnson "was heavier, his head usually shaved close. He dressed as neatly as he could, and the storekeepers along Forsythe remember him as a gentle, dignified man. During the winter, Angeline would lead him into the business district, and they would sing together in the noise and crowds of downtown Beaumont. Except for religious meetings like the encampment of the South Texas Missionary Baptist Association in Houston, they traveled very little."[30]

But according to Blind Willie McTell, Johnson did travel extensively. Willie Harris recalled that the two men met in April 1930,

Led Zeppelin's "Nobody's Fault but Mine" reintroduced Blind Willie Johnson's original song to a new generation of listeners. Courtesy Roger Misiewicz and Helge Thygesen.

when she and Johnson came to Atlanta to cut his final records. Three days earlier, McTell had recorded two songs of his own, "Talking to Myself" and "Razor Ball." It sounds as if Johnson had more influence on McTell than vice versa. For instance, at their 1935 Decca session in Chicago, Blind Willie McTell and his wife Kate performed several old-time gospel slide tunes reminiscent of Blind Willie Johnson with Willie Harris. In addition, McTell's 1940 Library of Congress performances of "I Got to Cross the River Jordan," "Old Time

Religion," and "Amazing Grace" shared a playing approach similar to that heard on Blind Willie Johnson's 78s.

During World War II, Johnson reportedly broadcast spiritual music over radio stations KTEM in Temple, Texas, and KPLC in Lake Charles, Louisiana. Michael Corcoran's research turned up a 1944 Beaumont city directory that lists a Rev. W. J. Johnson operating the House of Prayer at 1440 Forest Street, the same address that appears on Blind Willie Johnson's death certificate.[31] If reports are accurate, Johnson's death on September 18, 1945, was sad and avoidable. According to Angeline, he became ill after their house caught fire. "When we burned out, we didn't know many people, and so I just, you know, drug him back in there and we laid on them wet bed clothes with a lot of newspaper. It didn't bother me, but it bothered him. See, he'd turn over and I'd just lay up on the paper, and I thought if you put a lot of paper on, you know, it would keep us from getting sick. We didn't get wet, but just the dampness, you know, and then he'd be singing and his veins open and everything, and it just made him sick."[32]

Angeline took him to a hospital, where, she said, he was refused admittance. "They wouldn't accept him. He'd be living today if they'd accepted him. They wouldn't accept him because he was blind. Blind folks has a hard time."[33] Blind Willie Johnson's death certificate lists "malarial fever" as the primary cause, with "syphilis and blindness" as contributory causes. He was buried in the "colored section" of the Blanchette Cemetery in Beaumont.[34]

Over the years, Blind Willie Johnson's music has become deeply embedded in American culture. Its first inroads to a new generation came in 1950, when Folkways Records reissued "Dark Was the Night—Cold Was the Ground" and "Lord I Just Can't Keep from Crying" on their anthology *Jazz,* vol. 2, *The Blues.* Two years later, "John the Revelator" was included on Harry Smith's *Anthology of American Folk Music.* In 1957, Folkways issued *Blind Willie Johnson:*

His Story, the first album dedicated entirely to Johnson. Described on the front cover as "told, annotated and documented by Samuel B. Charters," this LP included the audio interview with Angeline Johnson.

During the early 1960s, Rev. Gary Davis taught Blind Willie Johnson's music to up-and-coming folkies. Davis's own versions of "If I Had My Way I'd Tear the Building Down," which he sometimes titled "Samson and Delilah," and "Keep Your Lamp Trimmed and Burning" inspired many subsequent covers. On his 1962 debut album, Bob Dylan recast "Jesus Make Up My Dying Bed" as "In My Time of Dyin'." Peter, Paul, and Mary recorded popular versions of "If I Had My Way" and "Go with Me to That Land," which they retitled "Come and Go with Me." "You're Gonna Need Somebody on Your Bond" was recorded by artists as diverse as Buffy Sainte-Marie, Donovan, Captain Beefheart, and Taj Mahal. During a 1992 interview, I asked Pops Staples about the guitar sound on vintage Staple Singers records. He picked up his unplugged electric guitar and played "Nobody's Fault but Mine." "Blind Willie Johnson," he said afterward with a smile. "That's where I got that from."[35]

In 1977 NASA launched its *Voyager 1* spacecraft to study our solar system and beyond. In case it's ever discovered by extraterrestrials, included onboard is a gold-plated disc containing images, videos, and sounds of life on earth. Its contents were selected by a committee chaired by Carl Sagan. Among its "Earth Music" tracks are selections from Mozart, Bach, Beethoven, Stravinsky, Louis Armstrong, Chuck Berry, and—you guessed it—Blind Willie Johnson's "Dark Was the Night—Cold Was the Ground."

Unlike most other prewar bluesmen, Lonnie Johnson specialized in urbane, sophisticated blues suitable for nightclubs and the concert stage. Photograph by Russell Lee, Library of Congress.

The Era's Most
Influential
Blues Guitarist

AS THE 1920S PROGRESSED, Lonnie Johnson emerged as the decade's most gifted and influential blues guitarist. Time and again, his uncanny dexterity, sophisticated sense of harmony, and brilliant solos enabled him to play in a wide variety of settings. He recorded classic jazz with Louis Armstrong and Duke Ellington, groundbreaking guitar duets with Eddie Lang, field-holler blues with Alger "Texas" Alexander, and plenty of blues, ballads, hokum, and pop under his own name. Even if he had never recorded again after 1929, Lonnie Johnson's place in blues and jazz history would have been assured. But he continued to make records—lots of them— through the 1960s.

Johnson's prewar 78s were especially popular among African American record buyers. "Lonnie Johnson has never been recognized as one of the transcendental people who influenced

Lonnie Johnson enjoyed one of the longest careers in blues history. Courtesy of the author.

everybody," says Ry Cooder. "You can recognize Lonnie Johnson in just about anybody, with his voice and elegant style. The stuff he did with Louis Armstrong is just incredible. What he must have sounded like to country black people! They must have thought, well, this is somebody else. He's uptown, getting this fabulous tone, and he's very elegant and top-hatted. It's a whole other thing. Pop music, really. You can see people copying him right and left. Oh, it's amazing."[1]

Johnson was city bred, and the majority of his original songs dealt with loneliness, insecurity, and the capriciousness of love and commitment. In Lonnie's blues, images like bedbugs and gambling became deeper metaphors of the disillusioned:

> *Love is just like playing the numbers,*
> *You got one chance out of a million time,*
> *You'll put your money on one-ninety-eight, and out pops one-*
> *   ninety-nine.* [2]

Lonnie could convey his humor and resiliency more easily through his fingers than his lyrics. Gifted with strong hands, a great touch, and a wonderfully fertile imagination, he could make his guitar thump like a country-blues starvation box or comp-and-fill like a piano. His crisp rhythms reveal a vast chord vocabulary, and his solos provide textbook examples of flawless articulation and superlative string bends. He had a way of beginning and ending songs with distinctive chord climbs, and with his brilliant right-hand technique and one-of-a-kind left-hand vibrato, he could approximate the sounds of a mandolin or bottlenecked guitar. Long, beautiful solos spooled out of him, conveying a sense that his hands were hardwired to his very heart and soul. Few guitarists—then or now—have achieved such an instantly recognizable style.

During the 78 era, Johnson overcame the limitations of primitive recording technology to achieve a consistent balance between treble and bass. He used a standard six-string guitar on his earliest recordings. Then, in the fall of 1928, he began recording with a twelve-string acoustic guitar. During the early 1930s, he switched back and forth between his twelve-string and a standard six-string, and from 1937 on played the six-string almost exclusively. His contemporary Big Bill Broonzy noted that Lonnie flat-picked all the time, but the simultaneous presence of bass notes during some of his treble-string passages suggests that Johnson played finger-style too. Before World War II, he usually played in the key of D, often using drop-D tuning (D A D G B E) and sometimes tuning both his low-E and A strings down a full-step while leaving the rest of the guitar at concert pitch.

Significant portions of the guitar vocabulary introduced by Lonnie Johnson have survived intact into the modern era. In terms of influence, he was surely the Jimi Hendrix of his generation. "Lonnie Johnson was the top guitarist," insisted Johnny Shines. "I remember one record of his was strictly jazz, and boy, he was so goddamned fast—whoo! With a straight pick. See, he use a straight pick like another man uses three fingers. I've seen guitar players use three fingers wasn't as fast as him."[3] Lonnie Johnson inspired countless prewar players to expand their dexterity and harmonic awareness, including Shines's friend Robert Johnson, who echoed bits of Lonnie's lyrics and guitar style in "Malted Milk" and "Drunken Hearted Man." Such was his admiration that in the early 1930s, Robert Johnson reportedly claimed on occasion that they were half brothers or that his middle initial, "L," stood for "Lonnie," when, in fact, it stood for "Leroy."[4]

Pioneering electric guitarists T-Bone Walker and Charlie Christian likewise drew inspiration from Lonnie Johnson's recordings, as would up-and-comers who began recording after World War II. Asked to name the blues 78s that inspired him in his youth, B.B. King responded, "My aunt used to buy records like kids do today, and some of her collection was Blind Lemon, Lonnie Johnson. She had Robert Johnson, Bumble Bee Slim, and Charley Patton. I could just go on and name so many she had. But my favorites turned out to be Blind Lemon Jefferson and Lonnie Johnson. I liked Robert and all the rest of them, but those were my favorites. There's only been a few guys that if I could play like them I would. T-Bone Walker was one, and Lonnie Johnson was another. I was crazy about Lonnie Johnson."[5]

In his 1996 autobiography, B.B. King further elaborated on his Aunt Mima's 78 collection: "Mima loved Lonnie Johnson and soon I learned to love him even more. It took a minute longer to appreciate Lonnie than Blind Lemon. Lonnie was definitely a bluesman, but he took a left turn where Blind Lemon went right. Where Blind Lemon was raw, Lonnie was gentle. Lonnie was more sophisticated. His voice was lighter and sweeter, more romantic, I'd say. He had a dreamy quality to his singing and a lyrical way with the guitar. Unlike Blind Lemon, Lonnie sang a wide variety of songs. I liked that. I guess he found the strict blues form too tight. He wanted to expand."[6]

In 1992, I had the occasion to play some blues 78s for John Lee Hooker at his home in Redwood City, California. When I spun Lonnie Johnson's 1930 recording of "No More Troubles Now," Hooker grew visibly excited. "Oh, boy!" he exclaimed.

> I love that man. I knowed him personally. Nice man. Like he just said [on the record], he like women, wine, and song. He got that style, man. He's blues and he's pop. There's some of everything, the way he plays it. Oh, I just can't say enough about the man. He was genius. And he had his own style too. He didn't sound like everybody that pick up a guitar. Nobody sound like Lonnie Johnson. You could tell it was Lonnie Johnson every time he picked it up. Oh, he could play a lot of notes, but you know who he was because he had his own style. Everybody loved him—black and white, wherever you are, they loved Lonnie Johnson.[7]

Alonzo "Lonnie" Johnson was born near Rampart and Franklin streets in the Storyville section of New Orleans, probably on February 8, 1894. At Johnson's final recording session, for Folkways Records in 1967, producer Moses Asch asked him about his musical background. "Well, in the first place, the whole entire family was musicians," Lonnie explained. "And I started to playing when I was fourteen years old. My father played music, my mother played music. My five brothers played music, and I had two sisters played music. And I just bought an instrument and in six months I was holdin' a good job. I was playing with my father's band—he had a string band. And we played for weddings and dances and private parties, things like that, dinners."[8] Lonnie's first instrument was violin, and in time he became adept with guitar, mandolin, banjo, string bass, and piano. His older brother, James "Steady Roll" Johnson, was also an accomplished multi-instrumentalist. Lonnie described how they'd perform together: "He played piano, and I played violin. And we'd switch. He would play violin and I would play piano. We made it, then I started playing guitar and he started playing violin. Then I would switch from the guitar to the violin, or he would play violin and I would play guitar. So that's the way it went."[9]

Growing up in New Orleans, the Johnsons were exposed to a much wider array of musical styles than country-raised performers could have heard. Visitors to New Orleans during this era reported hearing blackface minstrels, brass bands, string bands, symphonic musicians, voodoo chanters, hornpiping sailors, barrelhouse and ragtime piano players, carnival performers, and singers of everything from street cries to spirituals and opera. In the years before World War I, Kid Ory's band held court at Pete Lala's 25 Club, where King Oliver, Louis Armstrong, and other jazz pioneers would congregate. Members of Johnson's family played around Storyville, New Orleans's famed red-light district near the train station. Here, prostitution was available everywhere from cheap cribs to all-white brothels housed in mansions. Jazz flourished in its small taverns and clubs, but other styles were prevalent, too. Lonnie remembered,

"We played anything they wanted to hear—ragtime melodies, sweet songs, waltzes, that kind of thing. A lot of people liked opera, so we did some of that too."[10]

In his self-titled autobiography, pioneering jazz bassist Pops Foster remembered seeing the Johnsons performing on the streets: "Lonnie Johnson and his daddy and his brother used to go all over New Orleans playing on street corners. Lonnie played guitar, and his daddy and brother played violin. Lonnie was the only guy we had around New Orleans who could play jazz guitar. He was great on guitar. Django Reinhardt was a great jazz player like Johnson. They'd really take off on a number. Lonnie was tough to follow."[11] Lonnie also played established venues in the French Quarter, notably the Iroquois Theater, an African American vaudeville house, and Frank Pineri's club, which featured blues music. "I worked at the Iroquois Theater for a long time," Johnson explained to Paul Oliver, "and I worked at Frank Pineri's place on Ibreville and Burgundy. I worked down there, oh, God, I don't know, about four and a half years or something like that."[12]

In the Oliver interview, Johnson described how, when playing for himself, he especially enjoyed hearing the sound of his guitar reflected off water:

> When you tune it up, you got a beautiful instrument. And at night, if you want to get the right effect of it, take a small tub—you know, the smallest-size washtub. Fill it full of water. Sit out on the steps and put the tub of water down there. And you talkin' about a beautiful tone come from an instrument. You just sit there and play it and let that sound go to that water. And you talkin' about something beautiful! Oh, brother, I'm not kidding you. I'm talkin' about a feelin'. And it just goes, just goes . . . floats. The sound is better, softer, sweeter, travels further. It's more beautiful.[13]

When the U.S. military shuttered Storyville's sex establishments in 1917 due to public health concerns, Lonnie reportedly joined a musical revue that traveled to Great Britain. He is rumored to have performed for American doughboys in London and was reportedly seen playing banjo in Glasgow, but to date no one has turned up unassailable evidence of Johnson's war-era sojourn in Europe. In his Lonnie Johnson biography, Dean Alger writes, "It is probable that Lonnie was in London (and possibly elsewhere in Europe) roughly from the summer of 1917 until the summer or fall of 1919, returning to New Orleans at that time. A request for information in U.S. Army records on Lonnie's apparent service came up empty, but they said a fire some years ago destroyed a number of records from that time."[14]

Returning home after World War I, Johnson discovered that four of his brothers and all six of his sisters had perished in the influenza epidemic. His mother, father, and brother James were the sole survivors. "When I come back from overseas, I lost them all," Lonnie told Oliver. "And so then I started out on my own. I had to then—wasn't anything else to do. So I started to playing music for a living, and blues was all the go then, and I started to playing blues. From then on, I loved them, and I just continued to play 'em. And finally I got so I could make a living by singing the blues."[15]

Leaving New Orleans circa early 1920, Johnson never resided in New Orleans again, choosing instead to dwell in the big cities of the North. Later in life, he took umbrage when anyone referred to him as having rural Southern roots. Asked by Moses Asch what kind of music he played, Lonnie responded, "City blues. The blues that I write is from everyday life. See? The way people live, the happiness, the downfalls of life, and the beauty of life and living. The heartaches, the hardships, the crying, the happiness. And the other people that write blues, they write about the things that happen in the country—the chickens, the dogs, and the greens, and things like that. Well, I can't get it. So I write blues that people live every day."[16]

Lonnie and his brother James moved to St. Louis. Lonnie found work playing violin in Charlie Creath's Jazz-O-Maniacs, which

performed aboard the *St. Paul,* an excursion steamer on the Mississippi River. It's likely Johnson also played in St. Louis clubs between
riverboat excursions. Without recordings, he mostly relied on day
labor to stay afloat. He gave conflicting details about where he
worked and when, but it's possible that the East St. Louis steel mill
work he described to Moses Asch in 1967 occurred during his early
years in St. Louis:

> I started as a sand cutter and end up as a molder. I was molding these
> big boxcar wheels you see on the track—that's what I was molding.
> And I worked there for a long time. And I left there. They had a job
> open at the tie plant—you know, the creosote plant where they make
> railroad ties. So I went up there and I went to work. I didn't work there
> very long—I worked there six months because the work was too heavy.
> Those ties weighed from 150 pounds to 200 pounds, and only two men
> had to carry them, one on each end. And they come out of that creo-
> sote boiling hot, and you had those leather coats on. You put them on
> your shoulder, and you load 1,600, 1,700 ties into a boxcar. I got tired
> of that.[17]

To escape the drudgery of the mills and to gain wider recognition
for his musical abilities, Lonnie entered a 1925 blues talent contest hosted at the Booker T. Washington Theater on Twenty-third
and Market in St. Louis. Playing violin and singing, Johnson won
week after week, finally capturing the grand prize: an OKeh Records
recording contract. In the Asch interview, Johnson explained, "I'd
been on this contest for eighteen weeks—I won first prize every
Thursday night. Because it's hard to play violin and sing at the same
time, and I was doing that. And I was doing a very good job. And I
got a five-year contract from them. And I played violin and sang,
and my brother played piano for me. And I made so many beautiful
records for them."[18]

On November 2, 1925, Lonnie Johnson made his recording debut
playing violin and singing "Won't Don't Blues" with Charles Creath's
Jazz-O-Maniacs. Two days later, he made the first 78 released under

On his first solo release, Lonnie Johnson showcased the smooth, clear vocal delivery that would become his trademark. Courtesy Roger Misiewicz and Helge Thygesen.

his own name. OKeh Records, having not yet installed the new Western Electric recording process, captured this performance with the soon-to-be-obsolete acoustic method. With John Arnold rolling along nicely on piano, Lonnie began with "Mr. Johnson's Blues," playing hard and taking chances on guitar to lift a single-verse song into the realm of the sublime:

I want all you people to listen to my song,
I want all you people to listen to my song,
Remember me after all the days I'm gone.[19]

His smooth, clear delivery would become his trademark. For his second selection, "Falling Rain Blues," Johnson simultaneously sang and played fiddle. Because of the color of his skin, his 78s, like those of Louis Armstrong and Duke Ellington, were issued in OKeh's 8000 "race" series.

The sales of Johnson's initial 78 impressed OKeh executives, and in January 1926 the Johnson brothers traveled to New York City for a more ambitious set of sessions. Over a two-day period, Lonnie recorded nine songs under his own name, as well as two credited to his brother James. On their first selection, "Very Lonesome Blues," the Johnson brothers soloed simultaneously on violins. "Nile of Genago" featured them playing a lovely preblues parlor guitar duet. For his brother's debut 78, Lonnie played banjo on "No Good Blues" while James sang and played violin. On the flip side, James backed himself on banjo for "Newport Blues" while Lonnie used a kazoo or paper-covered comb to approximate a sassy horn part. At a follow-up session in St. Louis, James played guitar while Lonnie alternated between violin and guitar.

Johnson's 78s, which sounded unlike any other blues performer's, quickly found an audience. "Clearly, this was no ordinary artist," wrote Chris Albertson. "He was far more polished than the day's male blues singers, and his extraordinary instrumental skills matched those of the era's leading jazz players. Consequently, Lonnie began performing along the RKO and T.O.B.A. vaudeville circuits, outlets that remained closed to such contemporary country blues artists as Blind Lemon Jefferson, Papa Charlie Jackson, and Blind Blake."[20] A June 1926 ad in the *Chicago Defender* placed Johnson, who'd only been recording for seven months, in grand company. The evening's "Cabaret and Style Show" featured "OKeh Race Record Stars" performing a benefit for the Chicago Musician's Union. Among the musicians depicted in the ad are Sylvester Weaver, Bertha "Chippie" Hill, Butterbeans and Susie, Louis Armstrong, and Lonnie Johnson.[21]

In the Oliver interview, Johnson spoke of his time playing the Theater Owners Booking Association (T.O.B.A.) theater circuit:

> I worked on the T.O.B.A. from end to end. T.O.B.A. was just like any other theater business. You on the stage and you work and you do so many shows. At that time, on T.O.B.A., you work. You do five or six shows a day. Got a little money, but everybody was happy. I started on T.O.B.A. in Philadelphia—that's where I started from, the Standard Theater. I first had the band in the theater. Then after they put all of the live shows out, then I went on the road, travelin'. And I went as far as the T.O.B.A. could carry you—from Philadelphia to New Orleans [where] I played the Lyric Theater.[22]

He had fond recollections of meeting Clara and Mamie Smith on the T.O.B.A. circuit.

The Johnson brothers returned to New York City in August 1926, this time in the company of singer Victoria Spivey. "It was in the month of July 1926 that I met Lonnie Johnson in St. Louis," Spivey wrote decades later.

> I was introduced to him by Jesse Johnson of the Deluxe Record Shop [De Luxe Music Shoppe] on Market Street in the city. Jesse was a blues talent scout. This led to some record dates with Lonnie, who not only played guitar for me, but also violin on one occasion. . . . Lonnie Johnson had St. Louis sewed up with his brother James on piano. How many people know that Lonnie Johnson was considered the greatest violin player for blues in this world? I have great memories of him sitting on top of the piano, playing violin with brother James at Katy Red's in East St. Louis. Dollar, five-dollar, and ten-dollar bills would be flying as tips.[23]

SELL!

The Best
Popular
Vocals

SELL!

The Best
Popular
Dances

This can only be done by becoming Our Licensed Okeh Dealer

We all know them! Because they
are the greatest Race Artists

Butterbeans and Susie

Clarence Williams

Lonnie Johnson

Louis Armstrong

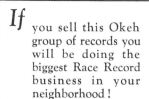

If you sell this Okeh group of records you will be doing the biggest Race Record business in your neighborhood!

Richard M. Jones and His
Three Jazz Wizards

Sara Martin

Consolidated Talking Machine Co.

227 W. Washington St.   Chicago, Ill.

BRANCHES: 2957 Gratiot Ave., Detroit, Mich.   1121 Nicollet Ave., Minneapolis, Minn.

At their first New York session together, Lonnie played guitar on Spivey's "Big Houston Blues" and violin on "Got the Blues So Bad." Lonnie then recorded eight songs as a leader, playing piano or harmonium on the first seven while James added violin. He concluded the session with "Sweet Woman, See for Yourself," playing guitar. The following day Lonnie recorded just one title, but what a doozy: the hyperkinetic guitar instrumental "To Do This You Got to Know How." OKeh's newly installed Western Electric recording process added depth and body to these initial New York recordings.

During the first half of 1927, Lonnie Johnson found plenty of session work. He and his brother accompanied Luella Miller on a dozen jazz and blues songs for Vocalion Records, with Lonnie stepping out on banjo, guitar, and violin. Lonnie and pianist John Erby accompanied Victoria Spivey on three OKeh-issued 78s, including the popular "T.B. Blues." Lonnie also played behind Helen Humes, Irene Scruggs, Bessie Mae Smith (aka "Blue Belle"), Raymond Boyd, and Joe Brown. At another St. Louis session, he backed a white performer, Alma Henderson, adding jaunty guitar to the pop tune "Red Lips, Kiss My Blues Away" and stately, string-bending blues fills to "Mine's as Good as Yours" and "Soul and Body (He Belongs to Me)."

That April, James Johnson journeyed out of town to play piano on Gennett 78s by Lizzie Washington, Henry Johnson and His Boys, Jelly Roll Anderson, and Katherine Baker. The guitarists at these sessions were identified as "Henry Moon" and "George Thomas," but audio evidence suggests that at least one of them was likely Lonnie Johnson moonlighting for a rival label. If so, these records would mark the final time the Johnson brothers recorded together. After

Seven months after his first recording, Lonnie Johnson was promoted alongside Louis Armstrong, Sara Martin, and others in this July 15, 1926, advertisement in *The Talking Machine World*. Courtesy Tim Gracyk.

the brothers parted ways in 1927, James Johnson devoted himself to club work. As Lonnie reported to Paul Oliver in 1960, James

> played piano and violin and guitar. He was better than me—holy smokes, yes. Yes, he's still living. He's in St. Louis now. He played the violin for Ethel Waters for I don't know how many years. That was her first violinist, my brother. He's been at one club there in St. Louis— it's in Newport, Illinois. He plays piano now, and he writes a lot of music. If I can remember closely, he's been there close to twenty-nine years—in that same club. He's still there—he is still there. It's called the Waterfront Club. I don't know why it's named that, because it's on the boulevard. But that's what it's called. And it's not near the Missis-sippi River, so I don't why—you figure it out.[24]

In August 1927 OKeh Records brought Lonnie Johnson to New York City for a three-month residency. He lodged in an apartment in Harlem and played sessions as both sideman and leader. On August 11 and 12, he made several memorable 78s with Texas Alexander, a cotton-field moaner with a powerfully resonant voice. Lonnie showcased a straightforward, sensitive feel for unadorned blues on the stark "Levee Camp Moan Blues" and "Section Gang Blues," essentially work songs with guitar accompaniment. Portions of the "Levee Camp Moan Blues" lyrics—"Lord, they accused me of mur-der, and I haven't harmed a man" and "They accused me of forgery, and I can't write my name"—would reappear in field recordings of Southern prisoners and in the repertoires of bluesmen such as Furry Lewis. Lonnie played more complex accompaniment on Alex-ander's "Range in My Kitchen Blues." While it isn't apparent while listening to his spot-on performances, Johnson found Alexander challenging to work with, as he explained to Paul Oliver: "He liable to jump a bar or five bars, anything. You just had to be a fast thinker to play for Texas Alexander. When you get out [of] there, you done nine days' work in one! Believe me, brother, he was *hard* to play for. He would jump keys, anything. You just have to watch him, that's all.

Start off singing just as nice, and all of sudden he'd jump keys. But I admired him. I got so use to playing for him. I didn't travel with him—I didn't travel at all with him. No. Just the recording dates."[25]

On the same days he worked with Alexander, Johnson also recorded five songs on his own. His voice confident and strong, he sang of the frightened and forlorn in "Lonesome Ghost Blues" and "Mean Old Bedbug Blues":

> *Something was moaning in the corner, I tried my best to see,*
> *Something was moaning in the corner, then I walked over to see,*
> *It was a mother bedbug prayin' to the good Lord for some more*
>   *to eat.*[26]

His "Fickle Mama Blues" delivered a message that would resound in many of his lyrics to come:

> *I got myself a mama, she's always got me feelin' blue,*
> *I got myself a mama, she's always got me feelin' blue,*
> *She act just like the weather, I don't know what she's going*
>   *to do.*[27]

He conveyed a more confident tone in his slow, emotion-drenched "Roaming Rambler Blues," singing of hopping trains and his success with women:

> *I got a gal in Texas, I got gals in Tennessee,*
> *I've got gals in Texas, I've got gals in Tennessee,*
> *There's a hundred doors fastened, waiting for this rambler's*
>   *key.*[28]

OKeh 8497—"Mean Old Bedbug Blues" / "Roaming Rambler Blues"— became one of his best-selling records.

In early October, Johnson teamed with pianist Porter Grainger for "St. Louis Cyclone Blues," in which he described seeing a cyclone from his shack's kitchen window, the howling wind toppling buildings:

> *The world was black as midnight, I never heard such a noise*
>   *before,*
> *The world was black as midnight, I never heard such a noise*
>   *before,*
> *Sound like a million lions when they turn loose their roar.*[29]

Perhaps Grainger based his lyrics on a real event. In 1896, the Great Cyclone of St. Louis killed 225 people and left a ten-mile-wide swath of destruction. For decades afterwards, booklets with photos of the destruction were sold around St. Louis. Johnson followed up "St. Louis Cyclone Blues" with "Bedbug Blues Part 2."

Johnson's next studio appearance paired him with Victoria Spivey for three days in late October and early November, when they recorded her classic "Dope Head Blues," the ever-so-dramatic "Blood Thirsty Blues" and "Murder in the First Degree," and several other sides. On Halloween, Johnson recorded two selections on his own, the guitar-piano instrumental "6-88 Glide" and "Tin Can Alley Blues," in which he sang of drinking "another half a pint and a good, cool can of beer." Lonnie Johnson wrapped up his New York dates on November 9 and 10 with "Bitin' Flea Blues," "Life Saver Blues," "Blue Ghost Blues"—one of his rare early recordings in the key of E—and an unaccompanied guitar solo, "Layin' on the Strings."

That December Lonnie Johnson was in Chicago, participating in one of the most important projects of his career. On Saturday, December 10, he sat in with Louis Armstrong and His Hot Five, playing music that likely conjured strong memories of his youth in New Orleans. The band featured Louis Armstrong on cornet, his wife Lil Armstrong on piano, Kid Ory on trombone, Johnny Dodds on clarinet, and Johnny St. Cyr on banjo. A bright twelve-bar blues sketched out by Lil, "I'm Not Rough," provided an ideal setting for Johnson's flat-picked tremolo and unsurpassed string bending. Midway through, the horns and piano dropped out, and St. Cyr comped

OKeh's "Life Saver Blues" advertisement featured a minstrel-style caricature of an African American man in distress. For decades, such unabashedly racist images were commonplace in the United States. Courtesy Thom Loubet.

quietly while Johnson played a beautiful single-string solo. Louis then sang a verse, accompanied only by guitar and banjo, and then the rest of the lineup swung into action in grand New Orleans style.

The following Tuesday, Lonnie joined Louis Armstrong and his band for another two songs. They began with the hard-swinging "Hotter Than That." Midway through the performance, Louis scatted along with Lonnie's guitar solo, and then engaged him in a series of exhilarating call-and-responses. The side concluded with a quick conversation between trumpet and guitar. Armstrong opened their final 1927 recording together, "Savoy Blues," with a vocal-sounding cornet solo. St. Cyr switched to guitar for this song, playing bass notes and comping chords beneath Johnson's exquisite solo. As Tony Russell wrote in *Masters of Jazz Guitar,* "To hear these three sides is to hear the turning of a page. St. Cyr was a well-respected musician and not an old man: he was thirty-seven and had a good few more playing years ahead of him. Johnson was only a few years younger, if at all, but in approach, technique, and even temperament, he belonged to another era, a Model T Ford to St. Cyr's horse and buggy."[30]

After finishing the Armstrong session, Johnson recorded four songs with pianist Jimmy Blythe for Gennett Records. The matrix numbers suggest that these sessions took place at a different studio. It's likely Johnson was moonlighting for a rival label, since all of his credited recordings to date had been made exclusively for OKeh Records. The label withheld "Handful o' Keys" and "Searchin' for Flats" from release, while "The St. Louis Train Kept Passing By" / "When a Man Is Treated as a Dog" were paired as Gennett 6366. The next day, Johnson and Blythe recorded an instrumental tour de force titled "It's Hot—Let It Alone," the more stately instrumental "Bearcat Blues," and the Johnson-crooned ballad "Why Should I Grieve When You're Gone." The 78s from these dates came out on the Gennett, Conqueror, and Supertone labels credited to a variety of pseudonyms—"Duke Owens and Bud Wilson," "Willie Woods and George Jefferson," "Sam Flowers, and Cloudy Williams"—but there's no doubt that the singer/guitarist is Lonnie Johnson.[31]

Johnson's Chicago sessions continued on Saturday, December 12, at OKeh's recording facility, where he covered Jim Jackson's hit two-part recording of "Kansas City Blues," which had come out on Vocalion two months earlier.

> *I got me a bulldog and a shepherd and two greyhounds,*
> *I got three high-yellows and three black and one brown,*
> *We going to move to Kansas City.*[32]

Lonnie Johnson concluded his Windy City sojourn four days later, accompanying Chippie Hill on four songs that were unissued.

We do not know how Johnson, a sensitive man who dressed sharply, had wonderful diction, and got along well with record company executives and musicians alike, felt when he saw OKeh's ads for his 78s. The graphic for his "Kansas City Blues" depicts him as a minstrel-style dandy, a Roaring Twenties version of old Zip Coon complete with bowler hat, dress jacket, striped pants, and oversized white lips. Leashes in his gloved left hand lead to the necks of three dogs and three nicely dressed women who trail behind. The copy proclaims: "He's a sly sort of fellow, dat boy is! Here he is. He got a Bulldog, one Greyhound, two Brownskins and one High Yellow. You can't do better than that, ole man!! He's takin' his way with wimmin' to Kansas City. Jes' hear that boy pleasin' with Kansas City Blues, parts I & II."[33] It wasn't the first time this type of imagery was used to sell a Johnson record: the "Life Saver Blues" advertisement had also featured a minstrel-style caricature of a helpless, coal-black man with oversized white lips rolling his eyes skyward as he drifts in a life preserver. Nor would it be the last.

By today's standards, these types of images and rhetoric, which appear in at least a half dozen other Lonnie Johnson ads, are

The advertisement for "Kansas City Blues" also featured an egregiously racist illustration to sell records. We have no record of how Johnson, by all accounts an intelligent, sensitive man, felt about these types of images. Courtesy Thom Loubet.

unabashedly racist. Common at the time, these images had been around for decades. OKeh was treading a fine line with Johnson, who was far more uptown and citified than other bluesmen. As Jeff Todd Titon observed in *Early Downhome Blues,*

> The record companies were among the first white American institutions to try to sell black Americans a product they could refuse to buy. Their advertising, while not surprisingly incorporating deep-seated racism, also revealed careful attempts to understand black people and their music. It exhibited the ambivalent feelings, ambiguous symbols, and contradictory activities which white Americans continue until this day. . . . Among white Americans—record industry officials were no exception—there was perhaps more anti-black feeling during the twenties than during any other decade since Reconstruction. The more emotional whites supported the powerfully resurgent Ku Klux Klan, while the intellectuals relied upon scientific support for their racism.[34]

As Titon points out, even the respected *Encyclopaedia Britannica* provided "scientific support" for racial inequality, declaring in its "Negro" entry, "Mentally, the negro is inferior to the white. . . . The mental constitution of the negro is very similar to that of a child, normally good-natured and cheerful, but subject to sudden fits of emotion and passion during which he is capable of performing acts of singular atrocity."[35] The acceptance of these stereotype-laden ads in the *Chicago Defender,* an African American newspaper that promoted racial pride, was probably due to financial reasons during the 1920s, since the newspaper's ad base consisted largely of record companies and cosmetic manufacturers.

But why were minstrel images applied specifically to someone as sophisticated as Lonnie Johnson, with his elegant style and fancy suits? Thom Loubet offers a compelling theory: "Record company promoters were in the awkward position of pursuing black consumers while still promoting their deep-seated racist beliefs about the place and function of blacks and black music. The solution, of course, was to conjure up images of the past—a time when life was simple and African Americans worked as sharecroppers on farms in the South, rather than competing for factory jobs in the North. Thus, distinctly urban musical expressions were marketed in terms of minstrel tradition."[36]

"The ads," Loubet continued, "powerfully support Titon's argument that the industry's marketing strategies grew, in part, out of a white fear of the rise of a black urban middle class. Lonnie was an especially large threat, and therefore the ads created for him were especially degrading."[37] In ads to come, Johnson would be paired with images of monkeys and baboons whose faces resembled his.

In his role of OKeh staff musician, Lonnie journeyed to Memphis in February 1928 to participate in a series of field recordings. He played guitar behind singer James "Mooch" Richardson, who would never record again. He played fiddle for guitarist Nap Hayes and mandolinist Matthew Prater, bowing a bouncy wall-to-wall solo in the danceable, good-time instrumental "Memphis Stomp." He drew a more mournful, countrified tone on "Violin Blues." Working with a singer identified only as Keghouse, Johnson provided stellar guitar solos on "Keghouse Blues" and "Shiftin' My Gears Blues." Playing alone, Johnson also recorded four important guitar instrumentals: "Playing with the Strings," "Away Down in the Alley Blues," "Blues in G," and "Stompin' 'Em Along Slow."

In his essay in *The Guitar in Jazz*, Dan Lambert cites "Playing with the Strings" as a classic example of Johnson combining elements of blues and jazz guitar and making it work:

> The basic structure here is an intro, seven choruses of varying length, a bridge, three more choruses, and the bridge again to wrap it up. The choruses range in length from roughly eight measures to roughly thirty—"roughly" because Lonnie frequently ignores the bar lines, changing chords at will, and any attempt to chart what he's doing rhythmically is at best an approximation. These irregular measures,

the general rushing of the cut time, the quick, upper-register melodies and descending diminished chords, all add up to give the tune a hot, zany feel. . . . Lonnie Johnson here has taken the abandon of primitive country bluesmen insofar as meter is concerned, adding the melodic variation and harmonic sophistication of a jazzman, and playing it all over a hot 1928 rhythm. It's a tune that stylistically bridges the gaps between blues and jazz, containing strong elements of both.[38]

Breathtaking displays of technical prowess and unstoppable enthusiasm, these four selections are among the best acoustic blues guitar instrumentals on record—wow!

From Memphis, the OKeh field recording unit moved on to San Antonio, Texas, in March 1928. In two days of sessions, Johnson backed Texas Alexander on eleven songs. He laced several selections with fancy flourishes and adapted a simpler, more down-home approach for others. A moaned work song, "Bell Cow Blues" was particularly effective. Johnson also recorded on his own, beginning with the vaudeville pop tune "I'm So Tired of Living All Alone." He returned to the blues for his four other selections. In the lyrics for the dropped-D-tuned "Broken Levee Blues," he assumed the persona of a man who's forced to leave his home to work on a levee—a very real issue in Mississippi and Arkansas in the late 1920s. When his character declares "I ain't totin' those sacks," the police put him in jail:

> *The police run me off from Cairo, all through Arkansas,*
> *The police run me off from Cairo, all through Arkansas,*
> *And put me in jail, behind those cold iron bars.*[39]

Johnson played a six-string guitar during all of these sessions. While in San Antonio, he explained to Paul Oliver in 1960, he acquired the twelve-string guitar that would soon be featured on his recordings: "I bought that twelve-string guitar in San Antone during the time I was playing at the Chinese Tea Gardens."[40] In a conversation

with Moses Asch several years later, Johnson further elaborated: "They only makes twelve-string instruments in San Antone, Texas. The Mexicans and the Spanish people—that's all they use is twelve-strings, twenty-four-strings, and forty-eight-strings. And they play 'em—I'm not kidding. So twelve is the best I could do."[41]

From San Antonio, Johnson journeyed to Dallas, where, on April 28, he was written up in the newspaper: "Lonnie Johnson, OKeh recording artist, has closed a very successful three-weeks engagement at the Ella B. Moore's Theatre. Mr. Johnson was booked for one week, but having proved so popular he was given an extension of two weeks. On the third and last week, a blues contest was given with Lonnie Johnson, Maggie Jones, Columbia artist, Texas Alexander, OKeh artist, and Lillian Glenn, the sensational new Columbia artist. Miss Glenn won as she is a local favorite, with Lonnie Johnson giving a close second."[42] A few months earlier, Lillian Glinn, as her name is properly spelled, had made her debut records with the same field recording unit that had recorded Blind Willie Johnson. While in Dallas, Johnson was paid one hundred dollars a week, tax free. While there, he met two other notable blues performers, Blind Blake and Jim Jackson.

In a photograph taken around this time, a dapper-dressed Johnson looks off to the side while holding a twelve-string guitar built around the turn of the century, probably by New Orleans luthier Rene Grunewald. It is uncertain if this is the guitar Johnson actually used or a photographer's prop. Paul Oliver asked Johnson about the twelve-string guitar he played during the late 1920s:

> I got more enjoyment out of the twelve-string instrument than I get out of the Gibson I play now [in 1960], because at that time I was

Lonnie Johnson with a twelve-string guitar, circa 1927. Soon after he purchased the instrument in San Antonio, Johnson played a twelve-string on classic jazz recordings with Duke Ellington. Courtesy of the author.

playing with my hands. I just used all five fingers in playing. I done a lot of solo work, and it was sweeter. The sound would come out more perfect, and I had my own way of tuning an instrument. All the strings wasn't tuned as a natural guitar. I had my own way of tuning. The first two strings is the E strings. Those was [tuned] correctly. They were all double. One G string was lower, and one was a tone higher than the other. And the D string was the same. And the bass string, the E sixth [string] was natural, but I had a G string next to it. With the lower pitch, it made a sound of an organ effect. It's a beautiful, beautiful tone. Right today, I wouldn't know how to tune it now. Believe me, I loved it. Oh, gosh. And you talkin' about a beautiful tone.[43]

Aural evidence suggests that Johnson may have occasionally modified the instrument into a nine- or ten-string by removing the octave strings from the lower courses or, alternately, from the B and/or high-E strings. Perhaps this was intentional, or it could have been the result of broken strings.

Johnson featured his twelve-string at his next session, with Duke Ellington and His Orchestra in New York City. The idea to team Johnson with Ellington reportedly came from Irving Mills, a shrewd manager impressed with Lonnie's strong record sales to African Americans. At the first session, on October 1, 1928, Lonnie introduced his new sound by exuberantly soloing through Baby Cox's tough scatting during "The Mooche," which could easily have underscored a graveyard sequence in an early Disney cartoon. Johnson delivered another unforgettable twelve-string solo in "Move Over," more than holding his own alongside the great horn men James "Bubber" Miley, Johnny Hodges, and Barney Bigard. In his final performance of the day, Johnson wove brilliant bends around Wellman Braud's powerful string bass in the fast-paced "Hot and Bothered." On the 78's label, OKeh credited "Move Over" and "Harlem Twist" to "Lonnie Johnson's Harlem Footwarmers."

At his next major session, Johnson recorded with the Chocolate Dandies, a big band fronted by the vocal trio of Don Redman, George

Thomas, and Dave Wilborn. Johnson played memorable twelve-string choruses on the slow blues "Paducah" and a show-stealing solo in the jazz standard "Stardust." He and Victoria Spivey also reunited for a series of vocal duets that were part skit, part seduction, and pure hokum. Spivey was at her sultry best in the two-part 78s "New Black Snake Blues," "Toothache Blues," and "Furniture Man Blues," fussing, cooing, and moaning innuendos at Johnson while Clarence Williams provided stately piano backdrops. For Spivey's "No, Papa, No!" Johnson tapped percussion on the back of his guitar. OKeh's "New Black Snake Blues, Parts I and II" ad declared it "The Most Sensational Race Record Ever Released! Two of the Most Famous Blues Singers are to be Heard on One Record. Mean! And How!" The graphic depicted two angry snakes, mouths open, menacing a pair of frightened, wide-eyed minstrel-style black faces.[44]

Lonnie Johnson returned to the studio on November 16 to record the first 78 featuring just his voice and modified twelve-string guitar. He revisited the themes of adultery and betrayal in "When You Fall for Some One That's Not Your Own":

> *A married woman will swear she'll love you all of her life,*
> *A married woman will swear she'll love you all of her life,*
> *And meet her other man around the corner and tell that same*
> *lie twice.*[45]

The 78's flip side, "Careless Love," a standard since the Buddy Bolden days, would remain in Lonnie's repertoire for the rest of his life. He explained to Oliver that he first learned the song in 1914 and added his own lyrics to it.

In November 1928 Lonnie Johnson and Eddie Lang began the collaborations that led to a groundbreaking series of guitar duets that would exert a profound influence on jazz guitar, then in its formative stage. The idea to team Lang, a studio sharpshooter who understood harmony better than any other jazz guitarist of the era, and Johnson, who had the finest technique in blues, originated with T. J. Rockwell, artist manager for OKeh Records. To mask the fact that the twenty-six-year-old Lang was white, the labels on the American releases of their original 78s credited "Lonnie Johnson and Blind Willie Dunn." Across the Atlantic, where there was a less-defined "race" market, Parlophone and Odeon correctly credited the sides to Ed Lang and Lonnie Johnson.

The son of Italian immigrants, Eddie Lang was born Salvatore Massaro in 1902 and grew up in South Philadelphia. As a child he studied violin. His father, a luthier, crafted his first guitar, which Eddie taught himself to play. He developed quickly, and by high school was playing duets with his lifelong friend, violinist Joe Venuti. In 1924 Lang had made his first notable recordings, "Tiger Rag" and "Deep Second Street Blues," with the Mound City Blue Blowers, essentially a white version of a jug band. Many sessions followed, and Lang became the top studio guitarist in New York City. By 1927 he'd recorded with Norman Clark, Irving Kaufman, Red Nichols and His Five Pennies, Bix Beiderbecke, Frankie Trumbauer, and many others. Venuti and Lang had also recorded their first of several violin-guitar jazz duets. He also made many solo guitar records under his own name, a

Eddie Lang, the leading studio guitarist of his era, joined Lonnie Johnson for a series of unsurpassed jazz guitar duets. Courtesy of the author.

standout being his knuckle-busting arrangement of Rachmaninoff's "Prelude." On record after record, Lang proved himself a master of articulation, harmony, and tone.

At the time of Lang's ascendency in jazz, most band rhythm sections featured a banjo player rather than a guitarist, largely due to the unamplified guitar's lack of volume on the bandstand. Lang had the skill and knowledge to bring the acoustic guitar to the forefront of the mix. George Van Eps, who knew Eddie Lang, told *Guitar Player* magazine,

> It's very fair to call Lang the father of jazz guitar. Who did he have to listen to? He had to develop his individuality by himself. His sound came from inside his head. Eddie didn't have anyone to copy. It always annoys me that Eddie is compared to players who came after him. It's terrible. Eddie was very progressive, and if he had lived longer than his short thirty years, he would have been as modern as tomorrow. He was a natural talent who made love to his guitar instead of beating it to death, which is what most guitarists tried to do. Banjo players *had* to switch to the guitar after hearing Eddie. There were a bunch of die-hards who tuned the guitar like a banjo, but he forced the issue and changed the sound of rhythm section.[46]

In the months leading up to his first collaborations with Lonnie Johnson, Lang had recorded with a variety of blues singers, sometimes displaying Johnson's influence. A few months after Johnson had recorded with Alma Henderson, for instance, Lang showcased his string-bending finesse on her "You Can't Have It Unless I Give It to You." Other dates found him paired with African American blues singers such as Victoria Spivey, Eva Taylor, and Gladys Bentley, whose "How Much Can I Stand?" and "Wild Geese Blues" foreshadowed the style of playing Lang would use to accompany Lonnie Johnson.

It's uncertain when or where the two guitarists first met, but on November 15, 1928, they both played on Texas Alexander's "Work

Ox Blues" and "The Risin' Sun." With Lang flat-picking chords and rhythmic figures beneath Johnson's heartfelt twelve-string soloing, they displayed an easy musical camaraderie. Two days later Johnson and Lang cut their first pair of guitar duets at the OKeh studio in New York City. Lang reportedly played his new Gibson L5 six-string archtop, while Johnson used his twelve-string. They jump-started the session with the energetic "Two Tone Stomp," with Eddie's complex bass lines and flawless chords supporting Lonnie's bluesy, happy melody—dig Johnson's fast triplets!

Johnson began their slower, twelve-bar "Have to Change Keys to Play These Blues" with a storytelling solo while Lang played bass notes and chords. Midway through, they briefly exchanged roles, Johnson strumming support beneath Lang's lower-register solo. Dan Lambert notes that Lang's solo is

> note for note the same break, though transposed, that he later played on Louis Armstrong's "Knockin' a Jug." Lonnie's playing here is very loose, very "off the cuff"—lots of smooth, bluesy flatted-third bends and descending chromatic scales. His guitar sustains nicely, giving his playing a distinctly human, singing tone. Lang's break, on the other hand, seems perfectly conceived and tight, and so the styles contrast to good effect—Lang's polished gem in the middle of Johnson's funk. The string bends in this tune are also of interest: Lonnie bends notes to make them "cry," wringing every last drop of emotion from a note, while Eddie bends notes to give them a slightly "off," out-of-tune sound. Lonnie's is the more emotional (bluesy) approach, Eddie's an intellectual (jazzy) approach.[47]

On most of their subsequent duets, Lang would focus on the rhythm role, supporting Johnson with innovative bass lines, arpeggios, natural and artificial harmonics, and a variety of extended, altered, and inverted chord voicings.

By 1929 the "hokum" fad was driving blues record sales. At the forefront were Tampa Red and Georgia Tom, whose songs "It's Tight Like That," "What Is It That Tastes Like Gravy," and "Pat That

To mask Eddie Lang's race, OKeh Records renamed him "Blind Willie Dunn" on the American releases of several Lang–Johnson collaborations. Courtesy Roger Misiewicz and Helge Thygesen.

Bread" are textbook examples of the zany style. At his first session of the year, in February, Lonnie Johnson tried his hand at hokum, recording the two-part vocal duet "It Feels So Good" with Spencer Williams and the single-sided "I Want a Little Some o' That What You Got" with Jimmy Foster. With their sprightly guitar and piano accompaniment, these songs are a far cry from the emotionally desolate blues "Death Is on Your Track" that Johnson and Williams recorded the following month. The advertisement for "It Feels So Good" featured a drawing of two monkeys holding a card with a photo of Johnson's face. The copy read, "It feels so good your heart's gonna start a throbbin', honey . . . there'll be sweet emotion a stirrin' yuh . . . when this greatest of all love songs takes you to a Garden of Eden."[48] The song became a hit, and three months later the duo recorded parts three and four.

In March, Lang and Johnson were both called in to accompany Louis Armstrong and his band. Lang went first, playing alongside Jack Teagarden and others on "I'm Gonna Stomp, Mr. Henry Lee." For the next two numbers, Armstrong brought in a new team of musicians, including Lonnie Johnson on guitar, Eddie Condon on banjo, Pops Foster on string bass, and Paul Barbarin on drums. Everyone but Condon was originally from New Orleans, and they raised the hometown spirit on "Mahogany Hall Stomp." Johnson delivered a superlative solo. As Larry Cohn, producer for Columbia Records, describes, "On this record, Lonnie Johnson was playing twelve-string guitar in a large band context as cleanly as one could possibly envision. Charlie Christian was fantastic, but Lonnie Johnson was doing it ten years before. He was a jazz musician nonpareil."[49]

At their next session together, on May 2, Lang and Johnson were joined by King Oliver on clarinet, J. C. Johnson on piano, and Hoagy Carmichael, who added percussion. The leisurely paced instrumental "Jet Black Blues" highlighted Carmichael's scat singing. Johnson soloed with aplomb on their other selection, "Blue Blood Blues." This lineup's only recordings, the 78 came out credited to "Blind Willie Dunn's Gin Bottle Four."

During the following two weeks, Lang recorded with Bessie Smith and joined Johnson for four guitar duets: "Guitar Blues," "Bullfrog Moan," "A Handful of Riffs," and "Blue Guitars." At their final meeting, on October 9, 1929, they recorded "Deep Minor

As the Roaring Twenties drew to a close, Johnson and Spencer Williams jumped on the hokum bandwagon with the two-part "It Feels So Good." Courtesy Thom Loubet.

Rhythm Stomp," "Midnight Call Blues," "Hot Fingers," and "Blue Room Blues." While Eddie provided piano-like rhythms and bass, Lonnie spun intricate melodies laced with fabulous pull-offs and bluesy bends. Johnson's fast, cascading triplet pull-offs in "A Handful of Riffs" and "Hot Fingers" were utterly brilliant and unlike anything heard before. Lang stepped out as lead soloist during parts of "Blue Guitars," "Midnight Call Blues," and "Blue Room Blues," while Lonnie seamlessly segued into rhythm. The improvisations capture the musicians' warmth, humor, and mutual admiration, and they're as fresh-sounding today as they were on the day they were recorded.

Lonnie Johnson fondly recalled Eddie Lang in an interview for the 1955 book *Hear Me Talkin' to Ya.*

> I well remember Eddie Lang. He was the nicest man I ever worked with. Eddie and I got together many a time in the old OKeh record studios in New York, and we even made many sides together with just two guitars. I valued those records more than anything in the world. But one night not long ago someone stole them from my house. Eddie was a fine man. He never argued. He didn't tell me what to do. He would ask me. Then, if everything was okay, we'd sit down and get to jiving. I've never seen a cat like him since. He could play guitar better than anyone I know. And I've seen plenty in my day. At the time I knew Mr. Lang, I was working for the Columbia record people in New York. That's all I did—just make sides. But the sides I made with Eddie Lang were my greatest experience.[50]

In between his final two sessions with Lang, Johnson recorded six songs on his own. As their titles suggest, "You Can't Give a Woman Everything She Needs," "From Now on Make Your Whoopee at Home," and "Baby Please Don't Leave Home No More" were sad blues about infidelity and abandonment. For "New Falling Rain Blues," Johnson put aside his twelve-string and played violin, adding a fill at the end of each of his vocal lines. In June, he and Victoria Spivey made their final prewar recordings together, the two-part "You Done Lost Your Good Thing Now."

As one of 1929's top race artists, Johnson went on the road with Bessie Smith's *Midnite Steppers* revue. Rumors flew when he was seen coming and going from Bessie's state room. "She was sweet on me," Johnson told Chris Albertson in 1959, "but we never got real serious. Bessie had too many things going for her."[51] Lang, meanwhile, put in time with the Paul Whiteman Orchestra and played sessions for Jimmy Dorsey, Hoagy Carmichael, Benny Goodman, Ruth Etting, Ethel Waters, and many others. He enjoyed an especially close musical relationship with Bing Crosby. Eddie Lang died in March 1933 from complications following a tonsillectomy.

In late October 1929, the U.S. stock market began to collapse, triggering an economic decline that led to the ten-year Great Depression. These events sent shockwaves through industries, the record business proving no exception. Midlevel performers saw not only their sessions dry up, but live bookings as well. Vaudeville, a steady source of live performances for recording artists, suffered another major setback with the concurrent rise of "talkies," as motion pictures with sound were originally called. A headline in a 1930 issue of the *Chicago Defender* said it all: "Hundreds of Performers Seek Bookings in Vain." In June, the managers of T.O.B.A. voted to close their theaters. "The blues ran out," remembered Thomas A. Dorsey. "It collapsed, seemingly, or the blues singers, they had nothing to do. I don't know what happened to the blues, they just seemed to drop it all at once, it just went down. . . . The artists were falling out because they couldn't get work. Well, there was just a slump on the record business after two or three years. It just seemed like the whole thing changed around, and there wasn't no work for anybody and they began to lose contact with each other. The record companies, they started publicizing some other types of music, see. [This started to happen] Oh, about 1929, 1930."[52]

Lonnie Johnson soldiered on, recording eleven new songs in January 1930. He changed his sound on the first two, "She's Making

Whoopee in Hell Tonight" and "Another Woman Booked Out and Bound to Go," playing a standard six-string guitar. Both were down-home laments along the theme of "If I catch you making whoopee on me, then you don't mind dying." Clarence Williams joined him for "Once or Twice," a guitarless pop song sung in unison, and the hokum songs "The Monkey and the Baboon" and "Wipe It Off." OKeh's ad declared that "The Monkey and the Baboon" was "Lonnie Johnson's Greatest Success. A new kind of Blues where you start with a laugh and end with a laugh. And it is full of the primitive power that brings people to the joy of love."[53] In the following months, Johnson and Williams recorded four more titles together—a watered-down version of "The Dirty Dozens," as well as "Keep It to Yourself" and a two-part "Monkey and the Baboon—Part 2," highlighted by Williams's falsetto horn imitations. Johnson also played on the Clarence Williams Jug Band's hot jazz 78 of "Sitting on Top of the World" / "Kansas City Man Blues."

Johnson was teamed with another notable artist, Clara Smith, Columbia's "Queen of the Moaners," on Halloween 1930. They role-played the parts of a nagging, unhappy couple on "You're Getting Old on Your Job" / "What Makes You Act Like That?," which came out on Columbia credited to "Clara Smith and Tommy Jordan." Their other collaboration, "You Had Too Much" / "Don't Wear It Out," was issued by OKeh as by "Lonnie Johnson and Violet Green." Johnson played a blazing solo in "What Makes You Act Like That?" but relegated his guitar to a supporting role on their other three songs. After this, Johnson's appearances as a studio sideman dropped off to the point where his sole assignment in 1931 was soloing on Leola B. Wilson's "You Need a Woman Like Me" and the Betty Boop–inspired "Boop-Poop-A-Doop."

He continued to record under his own name, producing nineteen 78s between January 1930 and August 1932. Among these were the enduringly popular two-part "I Got the Best Jelly Roll in Town." It's

OKeh Records declared "The Monkey and the Baboon" Lonnie Johnson's greatest success. Courtesy Thom Loubet.

speculated that Johnson himself played the ornate old-time blues piano on "I Have to Do My Time," "Southland Is All Right with Me," "Blues Is Only a Ghost," "Hell Is the Name for All Sinners," "Home Wreckers Ball," and "Sam, You're Just a Rat," none of which feature guitar. On the songs that did highlight his guitar prowess, such as "Got the Blues for Murder Only," "Let All Married Women Alone," and "Beautiful but Dumb," Lonnie relied on his twelve-string. He also turned in an exceptional six-string appearance on "Uncle Ned, Don't Use Your Head," a variation of "I'll Be Glad When You're Dead You Rascal You."

By now, Johnson was recycling chord patterns and melodies, counting on his lyrics to set his songs apart. Samuel Charters offered this explanation:

> His best records, sensitive blues like "You Don't See Into These Blues Like Me" or "I Just Can't Stand These Blues," sold poorly, but the thin, suggestive, or tasteless blues like "I Got the Best Jelly Roll in Town" sold much better. Some of his best-selling records were duets with Spencer Williams and Victoria Spivey that were as obscene as anything recorded in the 1920s: "It Feels so Good," "Toothache Blues," "Wipe It Off," "You Done Lost Your Good Thing Now." He was singing for an audience that was more interested in sexual suggestion than in music, and his best blues were too introspective and personal to reach many people.[54]

At his final 1932 session, in August, Johnson played a pair of maudlin ballads, "Unselfish Love" and "My Love Don't Belong to You," both issued by OKeh's parent label, Columbia. He followed this with a perfectly played guitar blues, "Go Back to Your No Good Man." Johnson's solo break in this song provides a superlative example of his poignant, well-controlled string bends and spot-on technique, but Columbia chose to shelve the song. Lonnie Johnson did not record again for five years.

For a while he worked as a laborer in a steel mill. As the decade progressed, he found work touring with headliners Glenn and Jenkins, who had a minstrel-style blackface routine: "I started to workin' on the RKO Circuit," he told Oliver.

> I worked from coast to coast on the RKO circuit: I played everything was playable—*every* theater it was. I was with the team of Glenn and Jenkins. I was with them four years. I split the [Glenn and Jenkins] act up and played music in between, singin' while they would make the change [of stage scenery]. This was in 1935, '36, '37, '38. And they went to England. I lost track of 'em. . . . . After that I was still playin' nightclubs, everyplace. I left from New York and went straight into Cleveland, Ohio. I started to playing in a nightclub there called The Heatwave. And it's still going. It's a big club—one of the biggest that is there. It's in the Majestic Hotel. I played blues. That's how it go. That's all [that's] goin' anyplace—if you don't know some blues, you just might as well forget it. You can play popular songs, anything you want all night, but somebody is goin' to ask you, "Play me some blues." And blues and the standard American jazz will never die. I don't care what they bring out—it'll live for a while, but it finally disappears. And they are right back to the same identical blues and American jazz.[55]

Sometime later in the mid- to late 1930s, Johnson headquartered in Chicago, where he played a variety of clubs. "First club I played in Chicago was the Three Deuces on North State with Baby Dodds on the drums and after that—lots of them. That's right. I played a couple of places on East 51st Street. I played at the Boulevard Lounge there on East 51st Street and then at Square's at 931 West 51st Street—I was there about five years, something like that."[56] Catching the attention of Decca Records, Lonnie Johnson, recording artist, was back in business.

During his first studio appearance for Decca, in November 1937, Johnson recorded eight songs with just his own guitar accompaniment. He was in top form, his playing tough and precise, his voice strong and confident. His first selection, "Man Killing Broad," revisited his old theme of betrayal:

You put Lysol in my gravy, black potash in my tea,
You put Lysol in my gravy, black potash in my tea,
But I fed it to your man, baby, instead of me.

Baby, I give you my money, I even let you run around,
Even give you my money, still let you mess around,
But you undoubtedly is the roughest little broad in town.[57]

He revealed the end result of this type of behavior in "It Ain't What You Usta Be":

You see, it ain't what you usta be, baby, it's what you are today,
It ain't what you usta be, baby, it's just what you are today,
You see, your good looks didn't hold your man,
And little black gal's lovin' stole your man away.[58]

Opening with a gorgeous guitar figure, his "Flood Water Blues" was an effective storytelling blues in the "St. Louis Cyclone Blues" tradition. The initial Decca session also yielded a pair of outstanding guitar instrumentals, "Swing Out Rhythm" and "Got the Blues for the West End," that are on a par with his classic 1920s instrumentals. During this period, a smiling Johnson was photographed onstage playing a Gibson J-100.

In other Chicago sessions, Lonnie demonstrated his flexibility playing solos in sax-driven ensembles. On November 8, 1937, for instance, he played on Ollie Shepard and His Kentucky Boys' jazzy "No One to Call You Dear (Ain't It Tough)" / "Sweetheart Land." At a Georgia White session the following day, he joined saxophonist Edgar Saucier, pianist Richard Jones, and an unknown drummer on three sax-heavy, forward-looking blues. Saucier sat out on their fourth selection, allowing Johnson to solo with aplomb on the rocking "Alley Boogie." He and pianist Blind John Davis also backed Merline Johnson for Vocalion.

At his final Decca session as a front man, on March 31, 1938,

Johnson played acoustic guitar. Most of his eight selections were straight-ahead blues laced with the world-weary lyrics familiar to longtime listeners. Set to bass, drums, and Roosevelt Sykes's driving piano, his "Mr. Johnson's Swing," however, told another story altogether. In the first verse, he sang:

> *I want all you people to listen while my guitar sings,*
> *I want all you people to listen while my guitar sings,*
> *If you ain't got that rhythm, it don't mean a thing.*[59]

Then, with an exclamation of "sing for me guitar," Lonnie launched into a blazing, breathtaking solo. In a follow-up verse, Johnson offered his fans an explanation of his five-year hiatus from recording:

> *Some people thinks I'm dead because I've been gone so long,*
> *Some people thinks I'm dead because I've been gone so long,*
> *I just stopped to see if you missed me from singin' these lonesome*
>   *songs.*[60]

Happy, up-tempo, brilliantly played, "Mr. Johnson's Swing" is nothing short of a tour de force.

The next day, Johnson played his first of three sessions backing East St. Louis's William Bunch, aka "Peetie Wheatstraw, The High Sheriff from Hell." In the session's standout track, Johnson used a six-string acoustic to energize the boogie-woogie "Shack Bully Stomp." Johnson's next session with Wheatstraw, on October 18, 1938, provides perhaps the earliest known example of Lonnie Johnson playing an electric guitar. His amp set on low, he delivered a scrappy, effective performance on their first selection, "Truckin' thru Traffic," playing his trademark style on what was essentially a new instrument at the time. He kept up the heat on five more songs with Wheatstraw, as well as on singer Jimmie Gordon's "Bleeding Heart Blues" and "Number Runner's Blues," recorded immediately afterward.

The electric guitar had, in fact, already been used for blues-oriented sessions in Chicago, but not many. It had first been featured at Western swing sessions. In 1935, for instance, Bob Dunn had played an electric steel guitar on Milton Brown and his Musical Brownies' "St. Louis Blues," and Leon McAuliffe had used an electric guitar on Bob Wills and His Texas Playboys' cover of Big Bill Broonzy's "I Can't Be Satisfied." The first person to play an electric guitar during a Chicago blues session was most likely George Barnes on Big Bill Broonzy's March 1938 recording of "Sweetheart Land" and "It's a Low Down Dirty Shame." Barnes, sixteen years old at the time, delivered a sophisticated performance with unusual string bends. Within a few weeks, he had also played electric guitar on sessions with Hattie Bolton, Blind John Davis, Jazz Gillum, Merline Johnson, and others. Barnes, who became an esteemed jazz guitarist, said in a 1975 interview, "When I was young, I hung around with Lonnie Johnson, and he taught me how to play the blues."[61]

At his next major sessions, in September 1939, Lonnie Johnson played acoustic guitar. The first of these sides was with Johnnie Temple, a Mississippi Delta blues singer in the Robert Johnson vein, on six songs set to a small ensemble featuring clarinet, piano, string bass, and guitar. During his solos in "Down in Mississippi," "Evil Bad Women," and a cover of Skip James's "Cherry Ball," Lonnie was woefully buried in the mix—if he'd only had an electric guitar at this session. The following day, Johnson accompanied Wheatstraw on six songs. Harmonica wailer "Rhythm Willie" Hood did the lion's share of the solos on these sides, while Johnson's parts were once again obscured in the mix.

Soon afterward, Lonnie Johnson joined Lester Melrose's stable of Bluebird artists. He commenced recording for the label on November 2, 1939. With powerful bass lines and dexterous treble fills, pianist Josh Altheimer, Lonnie's only accompanist on the date, helped create a fuller sound on Johnson's first four Bluebird 78s.

Using an electric guitar, Johnson approximated the sound of a slide guitar in parts of the ballad "The Loveless Blues" but stayed true to his acoustic style on the other tracks. These would be the only Bluebird records featuring Johnson on electric guitar. Mike Newton, an authority on early electric guitar recordings, has investigated why this occurred: "Years ago, I asked Homesick James why they didn't record electric earlier and without even thinking about it, he answered, 'Oh, Melrose didn't like 'lectric guitars.' Homesick wasn't the most dependable source of blues history, but I think he might have been telling the truth on that one. Lester may have been trying to keep his artists acoustic as long as he could."[62] At Johnson's subsequent Bluebird sessions, a string bass was added to the acoustic guitar-piano lineup.

Between recording dates, Johnson regularly appeared at clubs in Chicago. Charters reports that when the Three Deuces burned down in 1940, Johnson took a regular gig at the Boulevard Lounge on 51st Street. During January 1941 the Lonnie Johnson Trio, featuring Dan Dixon on guitar and Andrew Harris on string bass, made fascinating acetates during a gig at the lounge. Lonnie played piano and sang the straight-ahead blues "Falling Rain Blues" and "Rocks in My Bed No. 2," and soloed on acoustic guitar while Dixon strummed and sang "Secret Emotions." Lonnie also sang and soloed on a variation of "I Got Rhythm" titled "More Rhythm." In an early 1940s photo taken of the trio, a tuxedoed Johnson plays a Martin OO-21 acoustic guitar.

In studio sessions around this time, Johnson played on a pair of Clara Morris 78s, her only releases, and on the only 78 issued by Ruth Ladson and Three Shadows. He played some of his most outstanding parts while sitting in with Dixieland jazz ensembles, notably his acoustic guitar solos on Jimmie Noone and His Orchestra's "New Orleans Hop Scop Blues" and "Keystone Blues" and on Johnny Dodds and His Orchestra's "Gravier Street Blues."

In February 1942 Lonnie Johnson recorded his first R&B hit, "He's a Jelly Roll Baker." Soon afterward, war shortages brought a temporary ban on recording. Johnson went on the road, playing one-nighters throughout the Midwest and West Coast. Most of his income, though, came from outside of music. As he told Moses Asch, "I went and got a job at the country club, taking care of the grass on the golf course. I liked that. That was a good job."[63] He made his final Bluebird recordings—four songs with Blind John Davis on piano and Ransom Knowling on bass—in December 1944. His next appearance on record, in 1945, was backing singer Carl Jones and trumpeter Bob Shaffner on "Mitzy" and "Trouble in Mind" for Mercury Records.

In mid-1946 Lonnie signed with Disc Records, strapped on his

In 1941, Russell Lee photographed Lonnie Johnson's trio playing in a nightclub.
Photograph by Russell Lee, Library of Congress.

acoustic guitar, and cut ten tepid vocal blues and ballads with Blind John Davis on piano. Davis and Johnson found an easy camaraderie on the instrumentals "Blues for Everybody" and "Blues in My Soul," but overall this session was one of the most lackluster of Johnson's career. Johnson, again with Davis on piano, next cut two singles for the Aladdin label in June 1947, using an electric guitar for his extended solos in "Love Is the Answer" and the instrumental "Blues for Lonnie."

In late 1947 Johnson signed with Cincinnati-based King Records, a progressive independent label. Despite being located very near the South—Kentucky, where strict Jim Crow laws were still in effect, was just across the Ohio River—King Records had a nondiscrimination policy. African American, Asian, and white employees worked side by side and attended picnics, ball games, and parties together. In 1949, company spokesman Ben Siegel told the *Cincinnati Post,* "We pay for ability, and ability has no color, no race and no religion. Our hiring policy and our promotion system are based only on the question of the individual's capacity to fill a given job."[64] Johnson's label mates included gospel singers, country artists such as the Delmore Brothers and Grandpa Jones, and R&B stars Ivory Joe Hunter and Wynonie Harris.

At his very first session, on December 10, 1947, Lonnie Johnson recorded "Tomorrow Night." Set to piano and acoustic guitars, this tender torch song by Sam Coslow spent seven weeks at #1 in *Billboard*'s national Race Records chart. Johnson's biggest postwar hit, it remained in the charts for six months. For years afterward it was Johnson's theme song and a regular on juke boxes and at sock hops. "When he sang 'Tomorrow Night,' probably his most famous song," B.B. King remembered, "I understood that he was going to a place beyond the blues that, at the same time, never left the blues."[65]

For fans of guitar playing, the highlights from Johnson's first King session were the fleet-fingered, electrified solos on "What a

Woman"—the B-side of "Tomorrow Night"—and "Happy New Year Darling." In this latter song, Johnson, in a change of pace from his usual theme, sang of a man returning home from the war to find his wife's been faithful:

> *It seems like a long, long time since I've been fightin' the Japs 'cross the deep blue sea,*
> *Yes, it seems like a long, long time since I was fightin' the Japs 'cross the deep blue sea,*
> *Yes, that's why I'm so glad, darlin', to find the one I love still waiting for me.*[66]

Johnson was back on electric guitar at his second session, playing with surety on harder blues such as "What a Real Woman" and "Falling Rain Blues," a reworking of the song he'd recorded at his very first session in 1925. During the King Records era, Lonnie Johnson landed several singles in *Billboard* magazine's Race Records charts. As Jim O'Neal explains, "*Billboard* charts did not use the term R&B (rhythm & blues) until 1949. From 1942-1945 these charts were called the 'Harlem Hit Parade,' and from 1945 to June 1949 they were 'Race Records.' There were no relevant charts prior to 1942; otherwise some of Johnson's earlier records would have been chart hits too."[67] In October 1948, "Pleasing You," a ballad similar to the Mills Brothers' "You Always Hurt the One You Love," reached #2, trailed by "So Tired," #9 in 1949, and "Confused," #11 in 1950.

While researching his excellent blues history *Going to Cincinnati,* Steven C. Tracy discovered that during the King Records era, Lonnie Johnson and his wife, Kay, lived in a small house at 828 Rockdale Road in Cincinnati.[68] Tracy interviewed Roosevelt Lee, a musician who'd seen Johnson play across the Ohio River at the 33 Club in Newport, Kentucky. "He was a well-liked entertainer," Lee recalled, "and he would mingle with the people a lot. He would always— during intermission, he was always around people, laughing and talking, and very, you know, joyful, you know, very jolly. He wasn't what you call a guy that really belts out the blues. It was like a natural thing. It was tellin' a story, man, you know. The women and guys would really dig it because the lyrics was really about life."[69]

During his five years with King Records, Johnson recorded dozens of R&B-oriented singles, working with a variety of formats and backing. On one of the best, the swinging, sax-driven 1948 instrumental "Playing Around," he played a solo reminiscent of Charlie Christian's style with Benny Goodman. Working in a trio format, he delved into jump blues with "Nothin' Clickin' Chicken." He performed solo for "Backwater Blues" and "Careless Love," a man alone with the blues and an electric guitar. Backed by an accomplished big band with a hot horn section and kicking drummer, he poured his emotion into the burlesque-approved "I'm Guilty" and "You Can't Buy Love." Most of his King singles, though, were predictable, often beginning with the same opening—either a chord progression or one of his patented guitar riffs—and recycling the same chord progressions beneath his lyrics. As Johnson himself once claimed, "I recorded 125 songs against the same chords." After his final session on June 3, 1952, Johnson and King parted ways.

Three weeks later, Lonnie Johnson went on a tour of England, where there had been an interest in American blues ever since World War II. A recording was made of Johnson's solo set at Royal Festival Hall; the songs included "Stardust," "Just Another Day," "Backwater Blues," and "Careless Love." According to *Blues Records, 1943-1970*, Johnson also made a backstage recording with Lonnie Donegan and His Jazz Band, who had also performed that evening.[70] This tour was to be Lonnie Johnson's last major public performance of the decade.

During the ensuing years, Johnson resided in Philadelphia, where he worked as a janitor at the Benjamin Franklin Hotel. He regularly performed in the community and enjoyed giving lessons to young musicians. In 1956 he journeyed to New York City to record eight songs for the Rama label. Only one of his Rama singles featured blues—"Don't Make Me Cry Baby" / "My Woman Is Gone"—while the rest was pop fare, including covers of hits by Frank Sinatra and Les Paul and Mary Ford. These well-recorded singles brought him little acclaim.

His reentry into the mainstream blues recording scene came in 1959, thanks to Chris Albertson. At the time, Albertson was a dee-jay at WHAT-FM, Philadelphia's all-jazz radio station. He often played Lonnie Johnson's classic records, and one day asked on air what had happened to Lonnie Johnson. "The phone instantly lit up," Albertson recounted. "The first caller was banjo player and former bandleader Elmer Snowden—then a parking lot attendant—who himself was a legendary figure, having introduced Duke Ellington to Harlem in 1922. Elmer reported that Lonnie had lived in Philadelphia for the past several years, and that he had seen him at a

local supermarket the day before."[71] The Benjamin Franklin Hotel's maintenance supervisor confirmed that a Lonnie Johnson worked there but doubted it was the one who'd been a star. But, he told Albertson, "He might play guitar, because he's real careful with his hands and always wears gloves to protect them."[72] Albertson waited for Lonnie to report for his afternoon shift and knew at first sight it was the right man.

Albertson invited Columbia Records producer John Hammond and Riverside Records' Orrin Keepnews to meet with the newly "rediscovered" Lonnie Johnson and Elmer Snowden at his apartment that weekend. Both men showed up. With Albertson rolling tape, the musicians played and swapped stories. "It was an evening filled with amazing music," Albertson wrote. "Lonnie, the lean man with the misleading, perpetually sad face, looked much younger than his years."[73] When Hammond and Keepnews passed on recording Johnson, Albertson took the tapes to Prestige Records owner Bob Weinstock, who authorized new recordings.

Albertson's next step was to help the bluesman secure bookings and a good guitar. "I called the Willard Alexander office in New York City and was lucky to reach an agent who was an old Lonnie fan," Albertson explained. "The result was a three-week booking at the Chicago Playboy Club. I scraped together some money and bought Lonnie a tuxedo and a new Gibson guitar. I bought the guitar at Wanamaker's for around $600 and financed it through Beneficial Finance, so it took me years to pay for it! Lonnie already had an old guitar and amp, but neither was in good shape."[74] Lonnie Johnson was back in business. "I've been dead four or five times," he smiled, "but I always came back. This time, I knew that someday, somehow, somebody would find me."[75]

Lonnie Johnson toured Europe with the 1963 American Folk Blues Festival. Photograph copyright Val Wilmer.

At four sessions held between March and December 1960, Johnson recorded forty-eight songs. Bluesville Records, a subsidiary of Prestige, assembled these into four albums. Laid-back and expertly played, *Blues and Ballads,* with Elmer Snowden on second guitar and Wendell Marshall on bass, delivered just what the title promised. On the more ambitious *Blues, Ballads, and Jumpin' Jazz,* vol. 2, Snowden, who hadn't recorded in decades, played the fiery acoustic guitar solos in "Lester Leaps In," "C-Jam Blues," and "On the Sunny Side of the Street" while Johnson comped for him on an electric guitar. On *Blues by Lonnie Johnson,* the guitarist fronted a lineup of sax, piano, bass, and drums. *Losing Game* found him blending original blues with "Summertime," "What a Difference a Day Makes," and other standards.

During their time together, Chris Albertson gained insight into Lonnie Johnson's creative process. "I once asked him to compose a blues," Albertson recalled.

> It happened during the early days of our friendship. An advertising agency, having heard Lonnie perform on my radio show, asked me if he could write a one-minute blues to be used as a commercial for an auto insurance company. When I handed Lonnie a fact sheet with all the information they wanted included, he looked at it, said "Okay," and disappeared into the next room. A half-hour later he returned and performed for me a blues that lasted exactly one minute and contained all the facts I had given him—and it all rhymed perfectly. A superb writer who preferred to sing his own songs, Lonnie rarely resorted to clichés, but his melodic compositions offered less variety. "I play the same on a lot of my recordings," he said, candidly, "but most people don't realize it, because my stories are not the same, and usually people don't pay no attention to chords."[76]

Albertson's scans of the handwritten lyrics for this Rite-Way insurance company jingle reveal that Johnson had nice, legible penmanship.

Lonnie Johnson renewed his working relationship with Victoria Spivey. "We lost touch with each other until Chris Albertson and

Prestige Records brought us together for recordings in 1961," Spivey wrote. "I had Lonnie over to my home and we began to work on some new blues duets and songs which I wrote special for the occasion. Just like the old days in St. Louis! The first Prestige recording date in July with Lonnie was my first real one in nearly twenty-five years—and it gave me the go to go back in the recording biz. We cut two more sessions in September 1961 during the time we were working together at Gerde's Folk City in Greenwich Village. Two albums were issued—one called *Idle Hours*—Lonnie Johnson with Victoria Spivey—and the other, *Woman Blues*—Victoria Spivey and Lonnie Johnson."[77] The old friends resurrected the spirit of their 1920s duets on "Long Time Blues."

Lonnie Johnson playing an inexpensive Harmony Monterey guitar in 1960.
Photograph by Chris Albertson.

The experience inspired Spivey to form her own label, Spivey Records, located at 65 Grand Avenue in Brooklyn, New York. "From 1963 on," she noted, "Lonnie became practically a house man for my own record company. You can hear him sing and play on *Three Kings and a Queen* on Spivey LP 1004 and on *The Queen and Her Knights*—LP 1006—where Lonnie and I also added another duet to our wonderful history."[78] Another Spivey album, *Kings and the Queen,* also featured blues artist John Hammond with Roosevelt Sykes and a young Bob Dylan accompanying Big Joe Williams and Victoria Spivey. The following year Lonnie Johnson made two 45s in Cincinnati for King Records.

While these albums and singles are quite listenable, they did not gain Lonnie the 1960s mainstream recognition on the scale enjoyed by Mississippi John Hurt, Skip James, Rev. Gary Davis, and others who'd recorded before World War II. B.B. King, for one, found this situation disturbing: "As my life went on and my passion for blues grew, it hurt me to see that Lonnie never got the critical acknowledgment he deserved. The scholars loved to praise the 'pure' blues artists or the ones, like Robert Johnson, who died young and represented tragedy. It angers me how scholars associate the blues strictly with tragedy."[79] Part of Johnson's lack of mainstream recognition was due to the material he chose to play. Through Victoria Spivey, John Hammond, son of the Columbia producer, shared billings with Lonnie at Gerde's Folk City. "Lonnie wasn't playing much blues anymore," Hammond remembered. "He had just been found in a hotel in Philadelphia, and he sang some sweet gospel-type tunes and jazz standards. He'd lost that edge, but every now and then there'd be moments and flashes."[80]

Stefan Grossman, who studied with Rev. Gary Davis, remembers,

As a teenager I absorbed each word and note of Rev. Davis as the gospel. I bought blues albums, searched for old 78s, and went to clubs to see blues guitarists. Gerdes Folk City was a center for concerts in

New York City and one week I discovered Lonnie Johnson would be playing there. With great eagerness I went down to see the man Rev. Davis called "the king of the fret board." Lonnie was playing a cheap electric guitar and using a plectrum. His blues were a combination of late-1940s R&B tunes and folk blues played in a very diluted fashion. His singing had a cocktail lounge edge. All in all I was disappointed. I saw and heard nothing that I would want to play. During the next few years I saw Lonnie Johnson at various blues festivals and club appearances. I was never impressed, but in the back of my mind I had Rev. Davis' unequivocal recommendation that Lonnie was one of the best that had ever played the blues.

What a fool a teenager can be! If only one of my record collector friends would have played me some of Lonnie's great instrumental tracks from the 1920s, I would have been converted on the spot! As it was, I didn't really delve into Lonnie's playing until 20 years later. During the 1960s Lonnie's blues was out of fashion with both record collectors and blues enthusiasts. The Delta blues was high on everyone's minds and guitar-playing fingers. The steady flow of melodic riffs and runs that Lonnie recorded in the 1920s and 1930s were too sophisticated and jazz-oriented for blues guitarists and record collectors. Many of the finger-style blues guitarists of the 1960s eventually got interested in single-line improvisation and electric blues styles. This usually started with studying B.B. King and then Albert King and Freddie King. The road traveled backwards in time from players of the '50s and '60s—T-Bone Walker—to the '40s—Charlie Christian—and eventually ended in the '30s and '20s with Lonnie Johnson. The roots of modern electric blues and rock guitar can be found in the playing of Lonnie Johnson.

Lonnie was sadly overlooked in his later years by blues and guitar playing historians. He was never interviewed in depth about either his life or his guitar techniques. What a crime, especially as his guitar playing has so many mysteries. When listening to Lonnie's early great recordings, one is struck with how spectacular, complex, and innovative they are. What is very unusual is that the tonality and key is the same for so many tunes. He might have his guitar tuned low or play it with a capo or use a 12-string instead of a 6-string, but the chord shapes are always based around the key of D. Document Records released a seven-CD set, *Lonnie Johnson: The Complete Recorded Works,* and within these 140-plus tracks you will only find three or four tunes in a key other than D! Yet Lonnie's recording output in the 1940s and 1950s has little in common with blues in D and, in fact, he rarely played in that key or style during these years. I personally cannot cite any other guitarist whose style and technique changed so dramatically, especially when it was so widely acclaimed and imitated. This is a very strange phenomenon that only Lonnie could have helped us to understand.[81]

In November 1961, Chris Albertson read that the Duke Ellington Orchestra would be appearing at New York's Town Hall, and he asked the producer to arrange an onstage reunion. "He liked the idea and a deal was made," Albertson wrote.

> Lonnie would be featured as a soloist on one number, and it would be just like the old days. It wasn't. Lonnie was nervous, and we were both upset by a headline that appeared in the *New York Daily News* that day: "The Janitor Meets the Duke." Even when his career was at its lowest, Lonnie Johnson maintained his dignity and there was nothing cute about a headline that exploited his misfortune. The real reason why this brief reunion didn't produce memorable music was distance—Town Hall, 1960, was simply too far removed from the 1928 studio that sparked Lonnie and Duke's first collaboration. This was a different Ellington band and Lonnie's playing had changed a great deal. The sound of his electric guitar was conventional by comparison with the richly textured 12-string instrument that ignited the old versions of "Hot and Bothered" and, especially, "The Mooche."[82]

Nevertheless, John S. Wilson gave Johnson a glowing review in the following day's *New York Times*: "Lonnie Johnson, the veteran blues singer and guitarist, joined the band after the intermission and not only gave a useful demonstration of how to sing a potent and unpretentious blues but also developed what started out as a rather glib treatment of 'September Song' into a performance of such moving strength that even the usually implacable Mr. Hodges gave visible evidences of joy as he blew in the background."[83]

During September and October 1963, Johnson performed in seventeen European cities as part of the American Folk Blues Festival. The roster also included Muddy Waters, Otis Spann, Willie Dixon, Big Joe Williams, Sonny Boy Williamson II, Matt "Guitar" Murphy, and Victoria Spivey, who wrote, "I used to love to watch him stop the show with standing ovations."[84] In Copenhagen, Johnson and Otis Spann, longtime pianist for Muddy Waters's band, recorded material for an album released by the Danish Storyville label. Dressed in a fine gray suit, the dignified Johnson was also filmed on tour playing a mournful, unaccompanied acoustic version of "Too Late to Cry," punctuated with an adventurous extended solo.

Valerie Wilmer, on assignment for England's *Jazz Monthly* magazine, asked Lonnie to describe his style of blues. "I am altogether different from the rest of the people that sing," he responded.

> Some of them sing their words like it's country blues, and some of it is rock 'n' roll type singing. I sing city blues. My blues is built on human beings on land, see how they live, see their heartaches and the shifts they go through with love affairs and things like that—that's what I write about and that's the way I make my living. It's understanding others, and that's the best way I can tell it to you. My style of singing has nothing to do with the part of the country I come from. It comes from my soul within. The heartaches and the things that have happened to me in my life—that's what makes a good blues singer. Every State has its own style of singing, of course, but no one sings alike. I have my own original style, all my life I sang this way. I have also made quite a progress in singing ballads 'cause I sing blues, ballads, swing—anything. I have to do that in order to keep working 'cause some places don't like blues and then you don't have a job. So, whatever's happening, I keep up with the times.[85]

In the same interview, Johnson described his favorite guitar as "a late-style Kay [acoustic]. They make a light instrument that only weighs a little over two pounds and the execution on the fingerboard is so fast. You just have to touch it and you have no trouble playing it. I love it! I have a Gibson too, but I prefer that little fellow."[86]

In June 1965 John McHugh arranged to bring Lonnie Johnson, by bus, to Toronto, Ontario, for a two-week engagement at his Penny Farthing club. Johnson enjoyed Toronto so much that he spent the remaining years of his life living there. Bassist Jim McHarg, who fronted an energetic Dixieland band called the Metro Stompers, remembered in *Blues Access*: "Lonnie Johnson walked into one of the healthiest music environments in Canada ever—Yorkville in the mid-1960s. Folk music, traditional jazz, pop and rock all mingled

together in the same place, with everybody respecting each other and no rancor of any kind. We were all part of one big scene. The Metro Stompers were very, very successful there, and everybody loved Lonnie. Everybody."[87] John Lee Hooker echoed McHarg's sentiment: "When he lived in Canada, I'd go see him play. He was so friendly, with a nice personality. Always smiling. Everybody loved that man."[88]

For months, Johnson played at the Penny Farthing, knocking out audiences with his mix of jazz, ballads, and blues. "He was sort of a crossover artist who did everything he did very well," McHarg observed. "This didn't always sit so well with everybody. Some people might want to hear his instrumental side, and he would be singing the softer songs, or some people might want the blues thing. But Lonnie was always his own man. He would actually go in front of a blues audience and sing what they might see as a trite, sugary ballad. He would do what he wanted to do and sing what he wanted to sing. He was a free spirit, and I think that's one of the reasons why Lonnie loved Toronto so much—he was actually accepted as Lonnie Johnson. Not so many people tried to force him into a pigeonhole."[89]

Johnson especially enjoyed sitting in at clubs with Jim McHarg's Metro Stompers. In November 1965 Columbia Records arranged three hours of studio time for the musicians, which resulted in the tracks issued on the *Stompin' at the Penny* album. Johnson sang "Mr. Blues Walks," "Bring It Home to Mama," and "My Mother's Eyes." He took memorable solos in "China Boy," "West End Blues," and "Go Go Swing," which came as close to rock and roll as anything he'd recorded. "On Lonnie's recordings made in Canada with Jim McHarg's Dixieland band," described Larry Cohn, "he plays with

Lonnie Johnson spent his final years in Toronto, where he was embraced by a generation of younger listeners. Photograph copyright Val Wilmer.

the exuberance, stature, and command of a twenty-two-year-old. It's unbelievable."[90]

During a 1965 visit with his friend Bernie Strassberg in Forest Hills, New York, Lonnie sat down with someone's electric guitar and was taped playing a remarkable set of blues and jazz songs. He performed his own "New Orleans Blues," Bessie Smith's "Back Water Blues," Duke Ellington's "Solitude," Hoagy Carmichael's "Rockin' Chair," Frank Sinatra's "September Song," a seven-minute version of W. C. Handy's "St. Louis Blues," and other selections. While the sound captured by the Wollensak tape recorder is sometimes a trifle sketchy, the performances reveal Johnson's complete mastery of the guitar. In 2000, these performances were issued on CD as *The Unsung Blues Legend: The Living Room Sessions.*

Lonnie Johnson made his final recordings in 1967 for Folkways Records, playing an inspirational array of blues, pop, R&B, jazz standards, and rock-tinged songs and taping a four-minute interview called "The Entire Family Was Musicians." A lion in winter, Lonnie Johnson, now in his midseventies, still had it going on with both his voice and guitar. Performing alone, he sang with feeling and confidence, and fired off chorus after chorus of supple, perfectly placed solos. With the final track, he ended his recording career right where it had started, announcing into the microphone, "One more blues? Okay. I'll play you an old one I made a long time ago. I'll play you the first record I made for OKeh Records, 'Falling Rain Blues'—that was a big hit."[91] As the last notes faded, Lonnie Johnson concluded his forty-two-year recording career.

Lonnie Johnson returned to Toronto, where he'd spend the rest of his life. In 1969, while waiting at a bus stop on Avenue Road, he was seriously injured when a car jumped the curb and struck him. Ironically, he'd had a lifelong fear of automobiles. While in the hospital, he suffered a stroke that paralyzed his left side. After several weeks, Johnson was discharged. He was unable to play guitar again. When the bluesman felt well enough to face an audience, Jim McHarg and promoter Richard Flohill arranged for him to make an appearance at a Buddy Guy / Bobby "Blue" Bland performance at Toronto's Massey Hall. Flohill described the event in *Blues Access*:

> We brought him up from the audience, he sat on a stool, and Buddy Guy played acoustic guitar for him. Buddy very rarely plays acoustic guitar, but I remember how well he duplicated the style Lonnie had. So it was Buddy playing guitar, Jim McHarg playing bass, and Lonnie just singing. . . . Lonnie sang two numbers. He got a standing ovation, the audience was just so touched. You could not fail to be touched by this frail old man sitting on a stool with one of the hottest guitarists in the world playing acoustic guitar very gently and quietly and sinuously behind him as he sang these two songs. And when Lonnie left the stage, tears were pouring down his face.[92]

McHarg recalled that hundreds of young fans screamed their appreciation: "What a send-off! The audience was all young people, almost like a rock and roll audience."[93] This was to be Lonnie Johnson's final public performance.

Lonnie Johnson passed away in his apartment on June 16, 1970. Victoria Spivey published her eulogy in *Record Research*: "Lonnie Johnson was the greatest blues guitarist man in the business—and what a beautiful blues ballad singer he was too! Everywhere I turn, I hear him in T-Bone Walker, B.B. and Albert King, Muddy Waters, and the younger fellows like Buddy Guy. And, of course, all the white kids are playing Lonnie, most of them thinking they're being influenced by B.B. What I like about B.B. and T-Bone is that they all give Lonnie the credit for it. . . . I say to Lonnie: Join the heavenly Gabriel as you used to play with the earthly Gabriel, Louis Armstrong."[94]

MISSISSIPPI JOHN HURT

*Songster
and Bluesman*

MISSISSIPPI JOHN HURT had a gentle, guileless voice and a beautifully syncopated fingerpicking guitar style. After making a handful of 78s, he returned to rural Mississippi to farm and then arose phoenix-like during the 1960s, his considerable skills intact. Still fresh today, his inspiring recordings provide an aural passport to a bygone era of cakewalks and rags, ballads, and storytelling blues.

Hurt was thirty-five years old when he journeyed, guitar and business card in hand, from the Mississippi hill country to Memphis for his first recording session, on Valentine's Day, 1928. The experience was not entirely pleasant. Hurt remembered going into "a great big hall with only the three of us in it—me, the man [OKeh recording director T. J. Rockwell], and the engineer. It was really something. I sat on a chair and they pushed the microphone right up close to my mouth and told me that I couldn't move after they had found the right position. I had to keep my head absolutely still. Oh, I was nervous, and my neck was sore for days after."[1] Eight songs

Decades after his debut recordings, Mississippi John Hurt became one of America's most beloved country bluesmen. Photograph by Dick Waterman.

were cut that day, but only a single OKeh 78 was issued from the session, "Nobody's Dirty Business" paired with "Frankie," one of his songs in open tuning. Hurt was paid about twenty dollars per song, a good fee for unproven talent. The original Columbia file cards for the matrixes described them as "old time music," but this was later changed to "race."

Hurt headed home and worked another season. Under his share-cropping arrangement, half the corn and cotton he grew on thirteen acres was turned over to the landowner. In November T. J. Rockwell wrote to him, inviting him to record again. Hurt's December 21, 1928, session in New York City produced brilliant takes of "Ain't No Tellin'" (essentially new words set to the "Make Me a Pallet on Your Floor" melody), the murder ballad "Louis Collins," and "Avalon Blues," set to a galloping rhythm. A week later, Hurt had his final prewar session, cutting three spirituals and five blues. Of all Hurt's prewar sides, the one he composed his first day in New York City, "Avalon Blues," proved to be the most important. More than three decades after its release, it led to his rediscovery:

> *Avalon my hometown, always on my mind,*
> *Avalon my hometown, always on my mind,*
> *Pretty mama's in Avalon, want me there all the time.*[2]

During the 1920s, when its population was less than a hundred people, Avalon, Mississippi, was little more than a rail settlement on the edge of the Delta between Greenwood and Grenada. Born in nearby Teoc circa 1892, John Smith Hurt spent most of his life living there in poverty. His mother, Mary Jane McCain, was born a slave, and John and his eight brothers and two sisters grew up without a father. Hurt made it through the fourth grade at St. James School, and then began laboring for Felix Healey, whom he described as "a colored man" who owned a place across the way from his.[3]

Inspired by local musician William Henry Carson, John was nine

Hurt's 1928 recording of "Avalon Blues," a song about his Mississippi hometown, helped researchers find him in the early 1960s. Courtesy Roger Misiewicz and Helge Thygesen.

when he began teaching himself to play on a secondhand guitar his mother bought for him from a neighbor, Johnny Kent, for a dollar and a half. He described the guitar as being a "Black Annie" model.[4] "I always tried to make my strings say just what I say," he explained. "I grab it and go my way with it. Use my melody with it."[5] Resting his right-hand ring and little fingers on the face of his guitar, Hurt thumbed mesmerizing alternating bass lines while his index and middle fingers picked lilting melodies.

By age twelve John was singing "Good Morning, Miss Carrie," "Satisfied," "Frankie and Johnny," and other non-blues songs at house parties, sometimes working with a fiddler. "We had dances," he told Tom Hoskins. "We called them square dances. Hands up four. Ten gallons, oh, I don't know what you call these little dances. Why, they two-steppin'."[6] Some nights, he remembered, he and a friend would awaken neighbors with their playing, a tradition that had been part of American life for many decades: "We go along to people's private homes, way in the night, midnight, one o'clock. 'Serenadin',' we call it. We knew you well, we tip up on the porch and we'd wake you up with music. Well, you might lay there and listen, you might not get up and ask us in. Sometimes you'd get up and say, 'Come on in.'"[7]

In his conversations with Hoskins, Hurt described learning "Good Morning, Miss Carrie," "Salty Dog," and "Spanish Fandang" on the front porch of his shack. Asked about the first blues he'd learned, Hurt played "Lazy Blues," a simple, original arrangement in E major that had more in common with Memphis players than Delta musicians such as Charley Patton and Son House:

> *Wake up in the morning, a towel tied 'round her head,*
> *Wake up in the morning, a towel tied 'round her head,*
> *When you speak to her, she swear she almost dead.*[8]

Hurt also taught himself to play slide guitar. For his tour de force "Talking Casey," he'd thumb train rhythms on his bass strings while using a pocketknife slide to imitate bells and quote familiar melodies, a technique similar to Blind Willie McTell's. He composed in many keys, including E, A, D, and G, which was especially convenient for a strong alternating bass. But unlike many Delta musicians, Hurt seemed to prefer C, his key for "Make Me a Pallet on Your Floor," "Nobody's Dirty Business," "Richland Women Blues," "Louis Collins," "Let the Mermaids Flirt with Me," "Corinne, Corinna," and "My Creole Belle," among others. Big Bill Broonzy, who was raised in Arkansas, shared this trait. Hurt played harmonica, although later in life he was rarely seen doing it. Much of Hurt's music was probably a souvenir of his childhood. Asked how he developed his style, Hurt explained that he played "the way I thought a guitar should sound."[9]

In his youth, John helped his mother raise cotton, corn, and potatoes. As he grew up, he hired himself out to neighboring farms, while his mother washed clothes and cooked. Around 1915 Hurt worked for the Illinois Central railroad, jacking up and leveling railroad ties for one hundred dollars a month. His crew, he told Tom Hoskins, kept pace to a work-song rhythm—"callin' track," he called it. "Just one man keepin' time. Verses like 'Ida when you marry, I want you to marry me / Like a flower held, baby, you never see,' like that. I learned 'Spike Driver Blues' from a railroad hand called Walter Jackson. I just learned that song from calling track. 'Casey Jones' too." John quit the IC after five months, going back to help his mother on the farm. To earn extra money, he later cut and hewed oak, pine, and cypress trees into eight-foot cross ties to sell to the railroad at a dollar apiece. It was grueling work, he remembered: "I towed many a cross ties I made across my shoulder."[10] He married his first wife, Gertrude Conley, from whom he separated in the mid-1920s.

Around 1923 Willie Narmour, a white square-dance fiddler whose "Carroll County Blues" is still in the repertoire of many old-time musicians, began using Hurt as a substitute for his regular partner, Shell William Smith. A few years later, Narmour won a fiddle contest; first prize was a chance to record for OKeh Records. Arriving in Avalon to take Narmour to his field recording equipment in Memphis, producer T. J. Rockwell inquired about other local musicians. Narmour recommended Hurt and brought the OKeh executive to his shack. Hurt auditioned with "Monday Morning Blues," which led to his Valentine's Day session in Memphis. Of the eight songs recorded during Hurt's first session, only one 78 was issued—

Backed with "Frankie," "Nobody's Dirty Business" was the only 78 issued from
Hurt's debut session. Courtesy Roger Misiewicz and Helge Thygesen.

"Frankie" / "Nobody's Dirty Business." The "Mississippi" tag was
added to his name as a sales gimmick.

Hurt's follow-up sessions took place in New York City in December 1928. On the twenty-first, he recorded "Ain't No Tellin'," "Louis
Collins," "Avalon Blues," and "Big Leg Blues." "At that time they had
a large recordin' room," he told Tom Hoskins, "and they had a hallway between these buildings. Alright, you come out of the hallway,
you go in here, you recordin'. They keep the door closed, like that.

You could hear nothin'. The door, it was a glass door, you know, bottom was wood, and you could ease up to the door and peek through and lay your head close upside the door, you could hear like somebody way across town. But you weren't goin' to get in there till your time comes, see?"[11]

At his final New York session, on December 28, Hurt made his final eight prewar recordings, including "Stack O' Lee Blues," "Candy Man Blues," "Got the Blues Can't Be Satisfied," and the gospel tunes "Blessed Be the Name" and "Praying on the Old Camp Ground." While awaiting his turn, he met Victoria Spivey in a hallway and Bessie Smith coming out of an elevator. His most memorable meeting, though, was with Lonnie Johnson. "He had did some recordin' just ahead of me," Hurt recalled.

> Me and Lonnie, we was in the recordin' room there. I had just written this "Candy Man." I forget some of the verses, so they typed them on the chart, look and sing, so I was singin'. And so Lonnie see I was practicin' on it while they were gone. And Lonnie says, "Ain't that a little too high?" I say, "Yeah." He says, "Gotta be low. Gotta get it down, son." "High," I says, "high, right." I'll never forget the manager, T.J. Rockwell, come in and says, "Who's been messin' with that chart?" Lonnie says, "I did. I didn't think it would do any harm, it was too high." . . . We had us a little ball while we were goin'. I played the guitar, and he played the piano—oh, nice little ball. We went shoppin' or to his house, have a little party, dance. Oh yeah, had a big time.[12]

During the week between his studio appearances, Hurt saved most of his ten dollar per diem by taking room and board at the home of the man assigned to deliver him to a hotel.

Upon his return to Avalon, John Hurt settled into a quiet rural life with his second wife, Jessie Lee Cole, whom he had married in 1927. His records had little immediate impact on his career, but he still played Saturday night dances around Avalon, Carrollton, and Greenwood, sometimes working with fiddler Lee Anderson. While they were not strong sellers at the time of their release in the late

1920s, his 78s did influence other musicians, such as Doc Watson, who told *Sing Out!* magazine: "My first introduction to the blues was on the earlier recordings that came out with our first wind-up Victrola. This was about 1929 or 1930, and there was a record or two in there by John Hurt. I was just a young 'un, and his music struck a responsive note in me."[13] During the Depression Hurt worked for the Works Progress Administration (WPA), earning three dollars a day felling trees, building dams and levees, and cutting gravel roads. His WPA schedule of seven days on followed by seven days off enabled him to continue farming.

John Hurt never learned to drive a car and lived without electricity for most of his life. Around the end of World War II, he moved his family into a three-room house on A. R. Perkins's land, where he tended cows and farmed until the 1960s. Unbeknownst to Hurt, Folkways Records rereleased two of his old 78 sides in the early 1950s as part of its *American Folk Music* series, and he had gained a new circle of admirers who marveled at his appealing voice and dexterous fingerpicking. Most figured he was long dead, but Dick Spottswood, an authority on 78 records, had his doubts. He located Avalon on an 1878 atlas and shared his research with Tom Hoskins, a blues aficionado who headed to Avalon, population two hundred. Locals at Stinson's, which served as the community's general store, gas station, and post office, directed Hoskins to the third mailbox up the hill, where, sure enough, dwelled Mr. Hurt.

At the time, Hurt was earning twenty-eight dollars a month for herding cattle, cutting hay, and helping with cotton and corn harvests, while his wife cooked free meals for the farmer who owned their land.[14] Hoskins was thrilled to discover Hurt's musical skills intact. He talked him into coming to Washington, D.C., to begin a new career. "I thought he was the police," Hurt explained to *Time* magazine. "When he asked me to come up North, I figured if I told him no, he'd take me anyway, so I told him yes."[15]

In late March and early April 1963, Hurt recorded his first commercial LP. Produced by Dick Spottswood and originally released by the Piedmont label as *Folk Songs and Blues,* the album included recuttings of several of the OKeh 78s, as well as two of the first songs John learned as a boy, "Salty Dog" and "Spanish Fandang." In 1964, Piedmont issued a second album from these sessions, *Worried Blues.* Hurt recorded again in mid-July 1963, this time for the Library of Congress. The venue was Coolidge Auditorium, and Hurt's output—thirty-nine songs—rivaled that of two other great bluesmen who had recorded for the Library of Congress in the 1940s, Lead Belly and Blind Willie McTell. Hurt reprised many of his old 78s and pulled out his pocketknife for the slide effects in "Talking Casey Jones" and "Pera-Lee." Asked to play his favorite song, he launched into "Trouble I've Had It All My Days." Near the end of the session, he played a wonderful set of church songs that included "Beulah Land," "Oh Mary Don't You Weep," "Glory Glory Hallelujah," and "What a Friend We Have in Jesus." Before his final performance, Hurt said, "Let me do this one for you before we go. It's a love song, see?" John dedicated "Waiting for You" to his wife Jessie.[16]

Later that month, the sixty-nine-year-old gave his first major concert appearance at the 1963 Newport Folk

Mississippi John Hurt plays the Newport Folk Festival Workshop in 1965. Photograph by Dick Waterman.

Festival, appearing on a bill that included Brownie McGhee and Sonny Terry, John Hammond, Rev. Gary Davis, John Lee Hooker, Joan Baez, and Bob Dylan. Hurt's set included "See See Rider," "Stagolee," "Spike Driver Blues," "Candy Man," "Frankie," "Trouble I've Had It All My Days," and "Coffee Blues." The lamb went over like a lion, and afterward he graciously received his fans. Dick Waterman, who became his manager, remembers:

> When I saw Mississippi John Hurt at Newport '63, I was *profoundly* affected by him. He was all the good things. When you think of blues people, it's with a sense of sadness. But if you mention Mississippi John to Maria Muldaur or John Sebastian or Stefan Grossman, it's a smile. He was only around from '63 to '66—those three years. But he had so much! He was just such a positive guy. He was often quiet but really didn't miss anything. He would be sitting there, and people would be standing and talking, talking, talking, and John would look up and make a remark, and you went [*snaps fingers*], "Yeah! Of course." When he did speak, he really nailed it.[17]

After the Newport performance, Hurt headed home to pick cotton. He was soon back in the spotlight, though, triumphing at the Philadelphia Folk Festival a month later, with John Sebastian sitting in on harmonica for "Make Me a Pallet." Portions of Hurt's 1963 and 1964 Newport Folk Festival performances were released on the popular Vanguard Records anthologies *Newport Folk Festival 1963, Great Bluesmen at Newport,* and *Blues at Newport.* Hurt's 1929 OKeh records were reissued as well, initially on small-label anthologies, and then by Yazoo and Columbia.

John, Jessie, and their grandchildren Ella Mae and Andrew Lee moved to Washington, D.C., where they stayed in a third-floor apartment in a row house on Rhode Island Avenue NW. Rory Block was among those who made the pilgrimage to visit them there. "Mississippi John had recorded way back in the days of intense separatism," she says, "and then all of a sudden he was rediscovered by young white people, and he couldn't help but wonder what was going on.

He never expected that anyone would be listening to his music again, especially young white people, whom he never thought would be interested in his music. He appreciated it, though. He was very quiet, very thoughtful, and very sweet. He wanted to make sure you were comfortable, that you had a cup of coffee."[18]

Between concert appearances around the country, Hurt worked as resident guitarist at the Ontario Place coffeehouse. In less than six months, he'd seen his take-home pay jump from twenty-eight dollars a month to two hundred dollars a week. Hurt played Newport again in 1964 and went on to record several albums' worth of material for Vanguard, often in collaboration with producer and occasional second guitarist Patrick Sky. "John Hurt's music was so easily understood that everyone identified with him," Sky remembered. "And while there were many highly respected musicians during the '60s, John was the only one who was universally loved. To most of the folkies of the '60s, who were used to two and three chords on the guitar, his fingerpicking seemed like pure genius. I would say that John, along with Dave Van Ronk, were the most influential guitar pickers of the idiom during that time."[19] Van Ronk, in turn, praised Hurt for the inspiration he provided a generation of guitarists: "I count John Hurt as one of my best friends in music," he wrote. "He was a delightful man, charming and very easy to be with. And being with him was very much like listening to him. The most important thing about John as a musician was how playable most of his guitar work was. He was a brilliant arranger, but more important, most of his guitar arrangements were simple. That made his music accessible to beginning guitarists, giving several generations the kind of encouragement they needed to get started."[20]

With his angelic, wizened face and diminutive size (five feet four inches, without the old brown fedora), Mississippi John Hurt was as folkish and nonharrowing as his music. He rapidly became a cultural hero. "Hurt wasn't just a good musician," noted Dick Spottswood. "He had something which was very important in the 1960s. He had old record credentials, and he had been a legend for years. The myth was accessible instantly, and he had the music to back it up."[21] Rave reviews rolled in for Hurt's recordings and concerts. "The most important rediscovered folk singer to come out of Mississippi's Delta country, the traditional home of Negro country blues singers," proclaimed *Time* magazine.[22] Robert Shelton, writing for the *New York Times,* described, "At seventy-two, he is a country blues man, songster, and guitarist of compelling artistry. Far from being the primitive music maker one might expect to find in the hills at the edge of the Mississippi Delta, Mr. Hurt is a weaver of subtle, complex sounds. His performances have the quiet, introspective quality of chamber music, a welcome change from the younger folk musicians who think that 'loud' and 'fast' are all an audience can understand."[23] As Hurt's fame grew, he was booked into prestigious venues such as Carnegie Hall and appeared on the nationally televised *Tonight Show.*

Young musicians who became close to Mississippi John Hurt describe him as a wise and gentle man. "John Hurt was very Christlike and perfect," remembers Stefan Grossman, who studied guitar with him. "He had a repertoire of about eighty tunes, all of them gems. He was more of a songster than a blues musician, with a near-perfect guitar style. Onstage, he would rock back and forth with a little smile, very unlike someone like Son House. He was incredible, the storybook grandfather full of wise tales and wonderful stories."[24]

"Mississippi John Hurt didn't play really black music," Dick Waterman observes.

> In other words, he played a style that was an East Coast Piedmont style. It was more ragtime, like Blind Boy Fuller and Blind Blake and young Brownie McGhee. It's just when you're sixty-five, seventy years old, and people look at you and you're picking—well, he's been doing that for half a century. That's how he could do that. He was a magnificent instrumentalist. His speaking voice was very low and gravelly, but his singing voice was high and thin. And he had that innate, inexplicable quality to speak to everyone individually in the club, in the concert

hall, at the festival. He had that individual ability to just be talking to you. When he played, he always wore a hat. He lowered his head until his hat shadowed his eyes, so that there was no glare and he could see faces in the front. And he worked to faces. He worked to the individuals. He brought his head down until his eyes were shaded, and then he could see people. He was just a sweet man, a lovely, lovely man.[25]

Doc Watson echoed this sentiment: "John was one of the finest men that I have ever met. He was a kind, gentle-hearted person who loved people and loved life. And he enjoyed showing people his licks on the guitar."[26] John Sebastian, who named his rock group Lovin' Spoonful in honor of Hurt, was likewise deeply moved by Hurt's willingness to share his techniques. "John Hurt was the first blues musician to arrive in the Village with a very open attitude about sharing

Delta legends Mississippi John Hurt and Skip James backstage at the 1964 Newport Folk Festival. Photograph by Dick Waterman.

his guitar styles and licks," Sebastian told *Sing Out!* "It was like having our very own blues 'Yoda.' Whereas other musicians would hold back their tricks, except in concert, John would happily take you into the dressing room of the Gaslight and show you exactly what his hands were doing. We had all listened to his [1920s] performances, but another striking difference was that John had gotten better!"[27]

Then and now, countless guitarists have attempted to master John's seemingly "effortless" fingerpicking. "To a beginner," Stefan Grossman explains, "John Hurt seems really simple. He's playing like a piano, with treble on top of a boom-chick, boom-chick bass. But when you dissect them, every one of his arrangements has something unique. He'd stop the bass, or the bass wasn't where you'd expect it to be. He had unusual chord positions. He'd play set arrangements, but there would be little variations each time. He used three fingers to play, resting his ring and little finger on the face of the guitar while he fingerpicked. John's thumb strokes were the source of his unique sound. His alternating bass can stand by itself without any melody lines and still sound musical."[28] Luckily, excellent video footage survives of Mississippi John Hurt and his amazing hands.

Stefan Grossman observes that Hurt's choice of instruments seemed in keeping with his humble demeanor: "The Newport Festival wanted to buy John Hurt a guitar, so he came up to Marc Silber's Fretted Instrument Shop. We showed him a Martin OO-42, an expensive guitar with pearl inlays. And he just went for a simple Guild guitar that he picked off the wall. It was nothing special, not even a great-sounding guitar. It was very modest, just like he was. For his studio sessions at Vanguard, he used my OM-45 Martin, which happened to be an incredible sounding guitar. You can hear the difference between those recordings and the live Vanguard album that he did with the Guild."[29]

While Hurt seemed to enjoy his three years in the public eye, he grew increasingly unhappy with business dealings involving his music. "He got uncomfortable with people fighting to control his recording," Grossman details, "so he went back home and died in his sleep. He came in gently, left gently."[30] Mississippi John Hurt passed away on November 2, 1966. His funeral was held in St. James Church, and he was buried a few miles north of A. R. Perkins's house in rural Carroll County.

Long after Hurt's death, the legal battles continued. As Scott Baretta detailed in *Living Blues*: "A lawsuit over Vanguard's unauthorized release of Hurt's recordings eventually yielded nearly $300,000—none of which apparently went to Hurt's family—and the distribution of royalties due Hurt's estate was complicated by the fact that he apparently never officially divorced his first wife, Gertrude, with whom he had several children."[31]

In 2002, Hurt's granddaughter Mary Hurt Wright arranged to have his three-room dwelling moved from Teoc to nearby Avalon. It's now the Mississippi John Hurt Museum. Mary's grandmother, Hurt's first wife, Gertrude Conley, lived to be 111 and is also buried in the Hurt family graveyard. In 2004, the Mississippi John Hurt Foundation oversaw the installation of a state historical marker along Highway 7 in Avalon. It's inscribed, "John S. Hurt (1893–1966) was a pioneer blues and folk guitarist. Self-taught, Hurt rarely left his home at Avalon, where he worked as a farmer. Although he recorded several songs in 1928, including 'Avalon Blues' and 'Frankie,' he lived in relative obscurity before he was 'rediscovered' in the blues revival of the 1960s."

Over the years, many musicians have covered Mississippi John Hurt's songs, including John Fahey, Dave Van Ronk, Doc and Merle Watson, Bill Morrisey, Ben Harper, Steve Earle, Lucinda Williams, Alvin Youngblood Hart, John Hiatt, Gillian Welch, and Beck. To this day, Hurt's unique and accessible style continues to inspire players of all levels. I can't help thinking that Mr. Hurt, in his gentle, self-effacing way, would be pleased.

A master of hokum and an expert slide guitarist, Tampa Red skyrocketed to fame in the late 1920s. Courtesy of the author.

TAMPA RED

"The Guitar Wizard"

AMONG THE GALAXY of prewar slide guitar stars, none shone brighter than Chicago's Tampa Red. Bridging blues, jazz, and jive, his urbane, lighthearted records drew listeners from coast to coast. He was popular among record buyers for more than twenty years and released more 78s than any other artist in blues history. His influence stretched from Mississippi-bred bluesmen such as Robert Nighthawk, Muddy Waters, B.B. King, Earl Hooker, and Elmore James to Western swing bands and prescient rock and rollers.

With his warm, sweet tone and dead-on intonation, Tampa Red was a master of single-string melodies and streamlined chords—so much so that he came to be known as "The Guitar Wizard." He was also a terrific singer, with a keen, sensitive voice and streetwise delivery reminiscent of Lonnie Johnson, his favorite guitarist. Tampa Red's early ensembles were crucial to the development of Chicago blues bands, and several of the songs he composed or popularized ("Love Her with a Feeling," "Crying Won't Help You," "Sweet Little Angel," and "It Hurts Me Too" among them) have become blues standards.

"Tampa Red ironed out all the kinks," says Ry Cooder. "He made it more accessible and played it with more of a modern big band feeling—like a soloist, almost. He changed it from rural music to commercial music, and he was very popular as a result. He made hundreds of records, and they're all good. Some of them are *incredibly* good. You gotta say, okay, that's where it all starts to become almost pop. And he had a great guitar technique, for sure. He put it all together, as far as I'm concerned. He got the songs, he had the vocal styling, he had the beat. It's a straight line from Tampa Red to Louis Jordan to Chuck Berry, without a shadow of a doubt."[1]

Tampa Red was born Hudson Woodbridge in Smithville, Georgia, sometime between 1900 and 1904. Orphaned in his youth, he moved to his grandmother's house in Tampa, Florida, and assumed her last name, Whittaker. A boyhood bicycling accident permanently injured his foot, causing him pain as he got older. He took up guitar after hearing Mamie Smith's 1920 recording of "Crazy Blues," the first blues hit. "I didn't have no special teacher," he once said. "It was just a gift."[2] Inspiration came from a local musician named Piccolo Pete, as well as from his older brother, Eddie Whittaker. "Eddie didn't play the type of guitar I play," Tampa explained. "He played fingerwork, just straight guitar. He played Spanish-style, just natural chords."[3] Unlike the Hawaiian guitarists he'd seen playing lap-style, Tampa learned to play slide with his guitar held in standard position, using a thumbpick to strike the strings. "Instead of all that finger doublin' and crossin', I got me a bottleneck," he explained. "I used two, three, maybe four strings sometime. It's got a Hawaiian effect. I couldn't play as many strings as a fella playin' a regular Hawaiian guitar, but I got the same effect. I was the champ of that style with the bottleneck on my finger."[4]

Arriving in Chicago in his early teens, the diminutive redhead became known around town as Tampa Red, a reference to his light complexion. He sharpened his skills busking on the street, sometimes in the company of Sleepy John Estes and Hammie Nixon. He played a flashy, gold-plated National Style 4 round-neck resophonic in open D and open E, sometimes using a capo to change keys. With its three-cone design, the Style 4, a favorite among Hawaiian guitarists, created a smooth sound with longer sustain than the single-cone models favored by Delta bluesmen such as Bukka White. Johnny Shines, who knew Tampa Red, remembered that "his slide was just the tip of the bottleneck. It was very short."[5] In his autobiography, Big Bill Broonzy remembered meeting Tampa for the first time in 1928 and credited him with being the first person he saw play slide guitar: "A man like Tampa Red has got a style of his own, playing guitar with a bottleneck on his little finger, sliding up and down the guitar strings. He's the first one I've ever seen or heard doing that."[6]

Tampa Red made his first recording, "Through Train Blues," for Paramount in May 1928. In a feat he'd repeat countless times, he announced his unmistakable presence with his opening slide flourish—few players have ever achieved such an instantly recognizable sound. Set to tuba accompaniment, Tampa's debut was released paired with Blind Lemon Jefferson's "How Long How Long" on Paramount 12685. This would be the only Paramount 78 issued under Tampa's name. Paramount called Tampa Red back to the studio in September to back Ma Rainey, the South's most beloved blues diva. Tampa had met Ma's musical director and pianist at the session, Thomas A. Dorsey, a couple of years earlier. A self-effacing, schooled musician and prolific songwriter, Dorsey used the pseudonym "Georgia Tom" on blues records. At the Rainey session, Tampa Red held his resophonic guitar close to the recording source, his smooth, bittersweet tone perfectly complementing Rainey's powerful contralto. The four Paramount 78s the trio recorded together were among the final Ma Rainey releases.[7]

That same month Tampa Red and Georgia Tom began recording as a duo under the direction of J. Mayo Williams. In mid-September and early October they recorded the first takes of their new song, "It's Tight Like That," but these were deemed unworthy of release. On October 24, 1928, they successfully recorded the version released

Tampa Red and Georgia Tom's "It's Tight Like That" launched the hokum craze and became a best-selling blues 78. Courtesy Roger Misiewicz and Helge Thygesen.

as Vocalion 1216.[8] Accompanying his voice with strummed chords, bass runs, and a brief slide solo, Tampa sang the suggestive lyrics:

> *Now the gal I love, she's long and slim,*
> *When she whip it, it's too bad, Jim,*
> *You know, it's tight like that, beedle um bum,*
> *Oh, it's tight like that, beedle um bum,*
> *Don't you hear me talkin' to you, I mean it's tight like that.*[9]

Asked about the song's similarity to Papa Charlie Jackson's "Shake That Thing," Dorsey responded, "Yeah, well, 'Tight Like That' wasn't no original tune. It was just something that popped up at the right time, to make some money. It still goes! Tampa and, oh, it was a bunch of us, somewhere one night. And there used to be a phrase they used around town, you know, folks started saying, 'Ah, it's tight like that! Tight like that!' So we said, 'Well, that oughta work.' So we picked out a song. Tampa and I got the guitar, sitting around the house one night, at the dinner table there after dinner, and J. Mayo Williams heard it, and he said, 'Oh, man, we gonna record that! We gonna record that right away! Hold it right like that!' And so we did."[10]

"It's Tight Like That" quickly became one of the era's best-selling blues records. "'Tight Like That' went just about to the four corners of the United States," Big Joe Williams remembered. "Went through both races, white and black. You'd hear little kids mumblin' it everywhere you went."[11] Sixteen days after cutting their released duo version, Tampa and Georgia Tom went back into the studio to cut a rollicking version with kazoo, jug, jazz horn, and Frankie "Half Pint" Jaxon's unbridled vocals. This version came out credited to "Tampa Red's Hokum Jug Band." For the 78's flip side, the musicians cut an unforgettable cover of Leroy Carr's "How Long How Long Blues," with Jaxon moaning and cooing like a woman in the throes of orgiastic pleasure. For sheer salaciousness, Jaxon's performance was right up there with Lucille Bogan's unexpurgated "Shave 'Em Dry." Over the next two months, Tampa Red and Georgia Tom also cut "It's Tight Like That No. 2" and "No. 3" for Vocalion, as well as the irrepressible "Selling That Stuff" / "Beedle Um Bum," which came out on Paramount credited to "The Hokum Boys." On the Vocalion labels, the title "The Guitar Wizard" was added beneath Tampa's name.

"It's Tight Like That" helped spark the late 1920s fad for hokum, a zany musical style that set double-entendre-laden lyrics to jumping

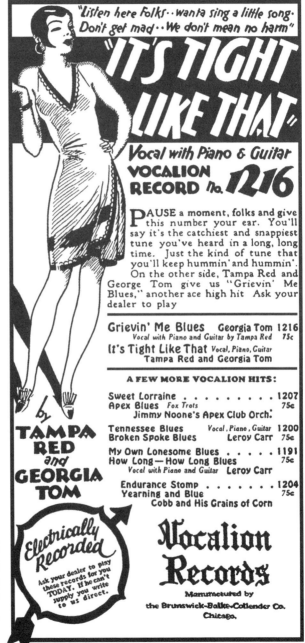

Vocalion Records used the image of a flapper to highlight the good-time nature of "It's Tight Like That." Courtesy Helge Thygesen.

good-time arrangements. The duo's success sent other artists scurrying into studios to wax what W. C. Handy referred to as "a flock of lowdown dirty blues."[12] Tampa Red and Georgia Tom cowrote dozens of songs, with both men supplying lyrics and Dorsey doing most of the arranging. On records, Tampa Red did most of the singing. "I'd push Tampa out there in front and let him do all the work," Dorsey explained. "I was the manager anyways. I said, 'You do the work!' Well, Tampa and I, we had some rough times too, trying to make it, but Tampa had something there, and he played a type of

Frankie "Half Pint" Jaxon sang the lead vocals on the Tampa Red's Hokum Jug Band 78 of "My Daddy Rocks Me." Courtesy Roger Misiewicz and Helge Thygesen.

Working as a studio musician, Tampa Red played superlative slide guitar on Lil Johnson's "House Rent Scuffle." Courtesy Roger Misiewicz and Helge Thygesen.

guitar that didn't many of the fellows play. I think he had something like a knife, or a piece of steel—something he run up and down that thing [with] which he made that whining effect in there."[13] The duo also played sessions together, backing Mozelle Alderson (aka "Kansas City Kitty" and "Jane Lucas"), Madlyn Davis, Octavia Dick, Bertha "Chippie" Hill, and Papa Too Sweet.

During 1929, Tampa Red made stacks of 78s under his own name and accompanying Lil Johnson, Cow Cow Davenport, James

"Stump" Johnson, Sam Theard, Romeo Nelson, and the Gospel Camp Meeting Singers. The uptown-sounding Tampa Red's Hokum Jug Band, which only came together as a studio unit, continued to make swinging, jazzy records like the raucous "My Daddy Rocks Me (With One Steady Roll)," which spotlighted Tampa's saucy slide and Jaxon's crazy asides. In another outstanding performance, Tampa played alongside pianist Charles Avery on Lil Johnson's "House Rent Scuffle," their hepped-up slide and driving boogie piano presaging rock and roll.

Between sessions, Tampa Red and Georgia Tom performed in public. "We'd play just anywhere," Dorsey reminisced, "party, theater, dance hall, juke joint. He was playin' on the street too."[14] Tampa experimented with bringing a rack-mounted kazoo into the act—a "jazz horn," as he sometimes called it—but Dorsey wasn't sold on the sound. "Tampa'd try any kind of thing if he thought he could get some publicity," Dorsey explained. "I'd tell him, 'If you gonna get a band, man, let's get a clarinet or a trumpet or somethin' now.' He'd say, 'No, we stay like what we are. We get all the money ourselves.' I said, 'That's all right with me.' He didn't use kazoo much then. I wouldn't let him use it much because he, well, sometime he'd get too much mind on the kazoo, and let down on the guitar, and that's the accompaniment, see. Instead of lettin' down on the kazoo—'Woo-oo-woo-oo-woo'—he'd stop strummin'."[15]

Traveling in Tampa's Ford automobile, the duo toured the black vaudeville circuit, playing theaters in Nashville, Louisville, and Memphis. During their October 1929 stop in Memphis, they played sessions with Jim Jackson, one of the most popular musicians in town, and Jenny Pope, who'd sung with the Memphis Jug Band. Tampa went over so well at the Palace Theater in Memphis, they asked him to stay over another week to perform solo. Back in Chicago, Dorsey commenced recording with Big Bill Broonzy and others. He explained to *Living Blues,* "You'd work with anybody if you could get to where they gon' get paid. Tampa and I were a steady team, but if I wasn't working tomorrow night and Bill wanted me, I'd go with Bill, see. Not only Bill, anybody. Frankie Jaxon or any of 'em."[16]

While the Depression brought a halt to most blues sessions, Tampa Red and Georgia Tom continued to record for Vocalion through the early 1930s, shifting between hokum, straight blues, and pop tunes. In February 1932, they journeyed to New York to make their final recordings as a duo and to work as session musicians for Memphis Minnie. Afterward, Dorsey announced his decision to concentrate on gospel music. "The blues started going down," Dorsey explained. "I said, 'Well, I'm goin',' and Tampa cried like a baby: 'No, Tom, don't go, look what, now look what we could do.' I said, 'Tampa, I'm gonna get into another thing. I'm goin'.' And Tampa cried like a baby: 'No, Tom, don't go. Now look what we could do.' I said, 'Tampa, you go with me, or else I ain't goin' no further. I'm losin' money, and I can't live. I can't eat and live with that.'"[17] During the ensuing decades, Rev. Thomas A. Dorsey, composer of "Precious Lord" and other classics, came to be known as the "Father of Gospel Music." In later years, he expressed fondness for his old partner: "He was a good fellow, good-hearted fellow. Never was in any trouble as I know of. Was never arrested or anything like that while I was with him, or never got in any fusses or any brawls or anything. Tampa was just as cool and calm as ever. He was a very nice fellow."[18]

For twenty-two months, Tampa Red made no recordings. He then concluded his tenure at Vocalion in March 1934 with "Black Angel Blues," which had been originally recorded by Lucille Bogan and eventually became known as the much-covered "Sweet Little Angel," and the poignant slide instrumentals "Things 'Bout Coming My Way" and "Denver Blues." That same week, he began his new association with producer Eli Oberstein and the budget-priced Bluebird label. Tampa's initial releases, cut with pianist Black Bob, featured a few slide gems, but he was beginning to recast himself

Georgia Tom Dorsey, seen here in the 1920s, went on to become Reverend Thomas A. Dorsey, composer of "Precious Lord" and the beloved "Father of Gospel Music." Courtesy *Living Blues* magazine.

as a crooner and kazoo soloist. By 1936, he was playing Leroy Carr-influenced piano on record, with Willie B. James sitting in on guitar. "I can play some piano, you know—ragtime, a little blues," Tampa said. "But guitar was my main thing, playin' 'Tight Like That' and 'Sell My Monkey.' I could do more with the guitar than I could with the piano because there was plenty of piano players who could play the real thing."[19] Following the pop trends of the day, releases by Tampa Red and the Chicago Five, a studio band with guitar, piano,

Tampa Red and Leroy Carr shake hands circa 1935. On record, Tampa's piano style reflects Carr's influence. Courtesy of the author.

string bass, and clarinet and kazoo (later replaced by sax and trumpet), were aimed at tavern jukeboxes.

Tampa Red turned his business affairs over to his wife, Frances, and their spacious home at 3432 South State Street became a haven for blues musicians. Blind John Davis, who accompanied Tampa on many recordings, remembered that Tampa's house "went all the way from the front to the alley. He had a big rehearsal room, and he had two rooms for the different artists that come in from out of town to record. Melrose would pay him for the lodging, and Mrs. Tampa would cook for them."[20] Tampa's pal Big Bill Broonzy was a frequent guest, and they enjoyed fishing, going to baseball games, and drinking whisky together. The Whittakers also hosted Memphis Slim, Willie Dixon, Jazz Gillum, Big Joe Williams, Sonny Boy Williamson I, Doc Clayton, Robert Lockwood Jr., Arthur Crudup, Washboard Sam, Big Maceo Merriweather, Romeo Nelson, Little Walter, Elmore James, and Robert Lee McCollum, who'd record as Robert Nighthawk. Tampa tutored Nighthawk, whose potent postwar electric slide merged his mentor's facile approach with a sustaining Delta whine. He rarely jammed with his house guests, preferring to relax with a drink and enjoy the goings-on. He worked hard at composing, though, scribbling notes on typewriter paper late into the night.

Blind John Davis recalled that when he first met him, Tampa had just composed a blues song based on an event in the news:

> At that time this Wallis Simpson and this Prince of Wales had just gotten married. And Tampa Red had made a number, "She's More to Me Than a Palace Is to a King" ["You're More Than a Palace to Me"]. So they take me over to Tampa's house, and Tampa had made this number. It was in a minor key. So Tampa's wife was sick at the time, in the bed. So when I got there, Melrose introduced me and he tells him, "Tampa, this man might can play your number." Tampa said, "No, I done had three or four guys up here, and they couldn't play it." So I says to Tampa, "Well, mister, play it. Let me hear a little bit of it, and

I'll see if I can play it." He played a little of it, so when I sit down, I played it. His wife hollered out of the bedroom. She said, "Tampa, that's the one!" He's the one that gave me my break, so ever since then, I been with Tampa.[21]

While Tampa Red occasionally toured in the 1940s, he mostly played around Chicago. For nine years he gigged just yards from his house at the H&T club, solo or in the company of Willie B. James or pianists Big Maceo, Sunnyland Slim, or Johnnie Jones, all of whom accompanied him on sessions. Tampa was one of the first Chicago musicians to acquire an electric guitar; audio evidence suggests that

Aural evidence suggests that "Forgive Me, Please" was Tampa Red's first recording on electric guitar. The song is credited to his childhood name, Hudson Whittaker. Courtesy Roger Misiewicz and Helge Thygesen.

the first time he used one in a studio was on December 16, 1938, for the session that began with "Forgive Me, Please." He turned in an especially memorable performance on electric guitar on 1940's "Anna Lou Blues," reworked by Nighthawk, Elmore James, and Earl Hooker as "Anna Lee." The same session yielded "It Hurts Me Too," later transformed into an Elmore James masterpiece, and "Don't You Lie to Me," which was covered by Fats Domino and Chuck Berry. Tampa appeared on Big Maceo's "Worried Life Blues" in 1941, and Maceo, in turn, manned the 88s on Tampa's 1942 hits "Let Me Play with Your Poodle" and "She Wants to Sell My Monkey." In 1945 Tampa Red moved from Bluebird to its parent label, Victor.

Although he was slowing down, Tampa Red stayed current, delving into horn-driven big-band jump à la Louis Jordan, power-house boogie-woogie, and as-yet-unnamed rock and roll. "When Things Go Wrong for You (It Hurts Me Too)," from 1949, made it into the national R&B charts. His last R&B hit was "Pretty Baby," recorded for RCA in 1951. Tampa Red added piano and drums to his club lineup and cut his final Victor sides in 1953 with a younger-generation band that included harmonicist Walter "Shakey" Horton, Johnnie Jones, and drummer Odie Payne. By then Tampa's uptown blues had been supplanted by the muscular rumblings of Sonny Boy Williamson, Little Walter, and Muddy Waters.

Approaching age fifty, Whittaker retired from the night life to care for Frances, who had a serious heart condition. Tampa's wife was "mother and God to him both," as Sunnyland Slim put it, and her death in 1954 left Tampa a broken man. He quit performing and escalated his drinking. Rumors of his erratic behavior began to circulate, and for a while he was confined to a mental hospital. "I got sick and had a nervous breakdown," he explained, citing his inability to refuse a drink as the cause.

He was coaxed out of retirement in 1960 to record two albums for Prestige/Bluesville, but gone were the slide gymnastics. Instead,

Tampa blew double-barrel kazoo and picked electric guitar counterpoint to his weary-voiced lyrics. After a few live performances, Tampa Red stowed his guitar beneath his bed. During the early 1970s, when labels began reissuing his old records on LPs, he was living on welfare with his companion, Effie Tolbert, on Chicago's South Side. He enjoyed sharing beers and hand-rolled Bugler cigarettes with old friends and the occasional journalist, but his recollections of his music career were few and far between.

After Effie Tolbert's death in 1974, Tampa spent his final years in Chicago's Central Nursing Home, where Blind John Davis looked after him. "Right now I'm Tampa's power of attorney," Davis reported in 1979.

> I bring him to my home about two or three times a month. I go and see him and see that he get his cigarettes, and he can have a couple cans of beer a day. So everything is beautiful that way. Well, he's in good shape. He's in beautiful shape. He's began to fool with his guitar again, and he's in good voice. So if he keeps improving, maybe in about the next six or seven months, we might come out with something. Man, if we do, we can almost write our own ticket. He's senile, and he don't remember too much, you know. But now if I start a conversation, he'd remember everything we talk about. But if I go to see him now and you go in the next fifteen or twenty minutes and asked him when he saw me, he'd say, "Well, I don't know when I saw John." It's one of those things.[22]

On March 19, 1981, Hudson Whittaker passed away. His gold-plated National guitar had been stolen years earlier, and his old Gibson electric went to Blind John Davis. He's buried in Mt. Glenwood Memory Gardens in Glenwood, Illinois. In his autobiography, Big Bill Broonzy had accurately predicted, "There's only one Tampa Red, and when he's dead, that's all, brother."[23]

Tampa Red playing over the radio with an electric guitar during the 1940s. Courtesy of the author.

Notes

INTRODUCTION

1. W. C. Handy, *Father of the Blues* (repr., New York: Da Capo, 1991), 74.
2. Perry Bradford, *Born with the Blues* (New York: Oak Publications, 1965), 14.
3. Ibid., 117.
4. Handy, *Father of the Blues,* 75.
5. Johnny Shines, interview with author, January 23, 1989.
6. Handy, *Father of the Blues,* 216, 218.
7. Jeff Todd Titon, "Living Blues Interview: Son House," *Living Blues,* March–April 1977, 18.
8. Jim O'Neal, e-mail correspondence with author, July 12, 2014.
9. Danny Barker, transcribed from the film documentary *Wild Women Don't Have the Blues* (dir. Christine Dall, Calliope Films, 1989).

SYLVESTER WEAVER

1. OKeh Records, advertisement for Sara Weaver's "Roamin' Blues," published in the *Chicago Defender,* January 5, 1924.
2. Nick Lucas, interview with the author, September 3, 1980.
3. Guido van Rijn and Hans Vergeer, liner notes to Sylvester Weaver's *Smoketown Strut* album, Agram Blues, AB 2010, 1982.
4. This ad for OKeh 8109 is reproduced in Jim O'Neal's "Guitar Blues: Sylvester Weaver," *Living Blues,* Spring 1982, 18.
5. Van Rijn and Vergeer, liner notes to Weaver, *Smoketown Strut.*
6. Robert M. W. Dixon, John Godrich, and Howard Rye, *Blues & Gospel Records, 1890–1943,* 4th ed. (New York: Oxford University Press, 1997), 547.
7. O'Neal, "Guitar Blues," 18.
8. Van Rijn and Vergeer, liner notes to Weaver, *Smoketown Strut.*
9. Mike Joyce, "Helen Humes: Interview," *Cadence,* January 1978, 6.
10. Helen Humes, letter to Guido van Rijn, June 15, 1980, reprinted in the *Smoketown Strut* liner notes.

11. Dixon, Godrich, and Rye, *Blues & Gospel Records, 1890–1943,* 1000. This track was eventually released on the *Smoketown Strut* LP as "Damfino Stump," and as "Damfino Stomp" on *Sylvester Weaver: Complete Recorded Works,* vol. 1, *1923–1927,* Document Records, DOCD-5112, 1992.

12. "What Makes a Man Blue," transcribed by the author from *Sylvester Weaver: Complete Recorded Works,* vol. 1.

13. "Penitentiary Bound Blues," transcribed by the author from *Sylvester Weaver: Complete Recorded Works,* vol. 2, *31 August to 30 November 1927,* Document Records, DOCD-5113, 1992.

14. Text transcribed from scan of original "Penitentiary Bound Blues" ad retrieved from the Internet. Original date and publication unknown.

15. "Chittlin Rag Blues," transcribed by the author from *Sylvester Weaver: Complete Recorded Works,* vol. 2.

16. "Railroad Porter Blues," transcribed by the author from *Sylvester Weaver: Complete Recorded Works,* vol. 2.

17. OKeh's "Black Spider Blues" / "Devil Blues" ad is reproduced in *Living Blues,* Spring 1982, 16.

18. Pen Bogert, interview with the author, January 10, 1997.

19. O'Neal, "Guitar Blues," 18.

20. *Chicago Defender* ad, June 12, 1926. This ad is reproduced in *Living Blues,* Spring 1982, 21.

PAPA CHARLIE JACKSON

1. Jim O'Neal and Amy van Singel, "Living Blues Interview: Georgia Tom Dorsey," *Living Blues,* March–April 1975, 20.

2. *The Paramount Book of Blues* (Port Washington, Wis.: New York Recording Laboratories, 1927), 25. This page is reproduced in *78 Quarterly* 1, no. 5 (1990): 15.

3. Norman Blake, interview with the author, March 10, 1988.

4. Paramount Records ad, *Chicago Defender,* August 23, 1924.

5. Robert M. W. Dixon, John Godrich, and Howard Rye, *Blues & Gospel Records, 1890–1943,* 4th ed. (New York: Oxford University Press, 1997), 23, 192, 495.

6. "Salty Dog Blues," transcribed by the author from *Papa Charlie Jackson: Complete Recorded Works,* vol. 1, *1924 to February 1926,* Document Records, DOCD-5087, 1994.

7. Dixon, Godrich, and Rye, *Blues & Gospel Records, 1890–1943,* 424.

8. Blake, interview.

9.   "Shave 'Em Dry," transcribed by the author from *Papa Charlie Jackson: Complete Recorded Works,* vol. 1.

10.   "Shake That Thing," transcribed by the author from *Papa Charlie Jackson: Complete Recorded Works,* vol. 1.

11.   Alex van der Tuuk, e-mail correspondence with author, October 21, 2014.

12.   "All I Want Is a Spoonful," transcribed by the author from *Papa Charlie Jackson: Complete Recorded Works,* vol. 1.

13.   Van der Tuuk, e-mail.

14.   Paramount Records ad, *Chicago Defender,* December 15, 1928.

15.   Derrick Stewart Baxter, *Ma Rainey and the Classic Blues Singers* (New York: Stein and Day, 1970), 44.

16.   Paramount Records ad, *Chicago Defender,* March 2, 1929. This ad is reprinted in Max E. Vreede's *Paramount 12000/13000 Series* (London: Storyville Publications, 1971), 12711.

17.   Paramount Records ad, *Chicago Defender,* June 8, 1929. Reprinted in Vreede, *Paramount 12000/13000 Series,* 12761.

18.   Van der Tuuk, e-mail, clarifies: "Since the studio in Grafton was not yet ready to be used, some of these early recordings are thought to have been recorded in a temporary studio in Milwaukee."

19.   Paramount Records ad, *Chicago Defernder,* February 22, 1930. Reprinted in Vreede, *Paramount 12000/13000 Series,* 12881.

20.   Samuel B. Charters, *The Country Blues* (repr., New York: Da Capo, 1975), 52.

21.   Van der Tuuk, e-mail.

BLIND LEMON JEFFERSON

1.   Stefan Grossman, interview with the author, February 22, 1992.

2.   John Hammond, interview with the author, July 25, 1990.

3.   B.B. King as told to Jim Crockett, "My Ten Favorite Guitarists," *Guitar Player,* March 1975, 22.

4.   *The Paramount Book of Blues* (Port Washington, Wis.: New York Recording Laboratories, 1927), 3. This page is reproduced in *78 Quarterly* 1, no. 5 (1990): 13.

5.   "United States Census, 1900," index and images, FamilySearch (https://familysearch.org/pal:/MM9.1.1/M3G4-749, accessed February 14, 2014), Lemmon Jefferson in household of Alex Jefferson, Justice Precinct 5 (all southeast of Big Tehuacana Creek), Freestone, Texas; cit-

ing sheet, family 52, NARA microfilm publication T623, FHL microfilm 1241636.

6. "United States Census, 1910; Census Place: Justice Precinct 6, Navarro, Texas"; Roll: T624_1580; Page: 17B; Enumeration District: 0098; FHL microfilm: 1375593. http://www.ancestry.com, 1910 United States Federal Census [database online]. Provo, Utah: http://www.ancestry.com. Original data: Thirteenth Census of the United States, 1910 (NARA microfilm publication T624, 1,178 rolls), Records of the Bureau of the Census, Record Group 29, National Archives, Washington, D.C.

7. Samuel B. Charters, *The Country Blues* (repr., New York: Da Capo, 1975), 57.

8. Ibid., 58.

9. Steve James, interview with the author, August 9, 1990.

10. Ibid.

11. Charters, *The Country Blues,* 60.

12. "United States World War I Draft Registration Cards, 1917–1918," index and images, Family Search (https://familysearch.org/pal:/MM9.1.1/KZX3-V2X, accessed February 14, 2014), Lemon Jefferson, 1917–1918; citing Dallas County no. 2, Texas, United States, NARA microfilm publication M1509 (Washington, D.C.: National Archives and Records Administration, n.d.); FHL microfilm 1952850.

13. Jonathan Black, "Draft Card Blues: A Newly Discovered 1917 Document Sheds Light on Blind Lemon Jefferson," *Living Blues,* October 2007, 67.

14. Ibid., 69.

15. Ibid., 71.

16. James, interview.

17. Charters, *The Country Blues,* 60.

18. Alex van der Tuuk, e-mail correspondence with the author, October 20, 2014.

19. "United States Census, 1920; Census Place: Kirvin, Freestone, Texas"; Roll: T625_1805; Page: 3A; Enumeration District: 24; Image: 235. http://www.ancestry.com. 1920 United States Federal Census [database online]. Provo, Utah, http://www.ancestry.com. Original data: Fourteenth Census of the United States, 1920 (NARA microfilm publication T625, 2,076 rolls), Records of the Bureau of the Census, Record Group 29, National Archives, Washington, D.C.

20.   Alan Govenar, *Meeting the Blues: The Rise of the Texas Sound* (Dallas: Taylor Publishing, 1988), 16.

21.   Gayle Dean Wardlow, interview with the author, 1989.

22.   Victoria Spivey, "Blind Lemon and I Had a Ball," *Record Research,* no. 76 (May 1966): 6.

23.   "Blind Lemon (Memorial Record)" and "Silver City Bound," transcribed by the author from *Leadbelly: Complete Recorded Works 1939-1947,* vol. 3, *October 1943 to 25 April 1944,* Document Records, DOCD-5228, 1994.

24.   Transcribed by the author from *Lead Belly's Last Sessions,* Folkways Records, SFW40068, 1994.

25.   Walker quoted in Govenar, *Meeting the Blues,* 45.

26.   Jim O'Neal and Amy van Singel, "Living Blues Interview: T-Bone Walker," *Living Blues,* Winter 1972-73, 20-21.

27.   Lipscomb quoted in Govenar, *Meeting the Blues,* 24.

28.   Robert M. W. Dixon, John Godrich, and Howard Rye, *Blues & Gospel Records, 1890-1943,* 4th ed. (New York: Oxford University Press, 1997), 442.

29.   Paramount Records ad, *Chicago Defender,* April 3, 1926.

30.   Williams quoted in Alan B. Govenar and Jay F. Brakefield, *Deep Ellum: The Other Side of Dallas* (College Station: Texas A&M University Press, 2013), 98.

31.   "That Black Snake Moan," transcribed by the author from *Blind Lemon Jefferson: Complete Recorded Works,* vol. 2, *1927,* Document Records, DOCD-5018, 2002.

32.   Roger S. Brown, "Recording Pioneer Polk Brockman," *Living Blues,* September-October 1975, 31.

33.   Ibid.

34.   B.B. King, interview with Billy Gibbons and Jas Obrecht, April 9, 1991. Quotation first published in "B.B. & Billy: Memphis and the Early Years," *Guitar Player,* June 1991. Complete interview reprinted in Jas Obrecht, ed., *Rollin' & Tumblin': The Postwar Blues Guitarists* (San Francisco: Miller Freeman Books, 2000), 330-44.

35.   Nick Perls, letter to the author, March 14, 1986.

36.   Holcomb quoted in Tony Russell, *Blacks, Whites, and Blues* (New York: Stein & Day, 1970), 48.

37.   James, interview.

38. King, interview.

39. Tom Wheeler, "Michael Bloomfield: Barroom Scholar of the Blues, *Guitar Player,* April 1979, 68.

40. James, interview.

41. Grossman, interview.

42. "Rambler Blues," transcribed by the author from *Blind Lemon Jefferson: Complete Recorded Works,* vol. 2.

43. "Rambler Blues" ad in *Chicago Defender,* original publication date unknown.

44. Smith quoted in Russell, *Blacks, Whites, and Blues,* 48.

45. Dan Forte, "Albert King: Power Blues," *Guitar Player,* September 1977, 38.

46. Wardlow, interview.

47. Stephen Calt and Gayle Wardlow, *King of the Delta Blues: The Life and Music of Charlie Patton* (Newton, N.J.: Rock Chapel Press, 1988), 177.

48. David Evans, "Rubin Lacy," in *Nothing but the Blues,* ed. Mike Leadbitter (London: Oak Publications, 1971), 242.

49. Ishmon Bracey, interview with Gayle Dean Wardlow, transcription mailed to the author in 1989.

50. Jim O'Neal, "Living Blues Interview: Houston Stackhouse," *Living Blues,* Summer 1974, 21.

51. Ibid.

52. "Saturday Night Spender Blues," "Black Snake Moan No. 2," and "Bakershop Blues," transcribed by the author from *Blind Lemon Jefferson: Complete Recorded Works,* vol. 4, *1929,* Document Records, DOCD-5020, 2000.

53. Wheeler, "Michael Bloomfield," 68.

54. Wardlow, interview.

55. "Wasn't It Sad about Lemon" and "Death of Blind Lemon," transcribed by the author from Walter and Byrd's "Wasn't It Sad about Lemon," Paramount 12945, 1930.

56. Van der Tuuk, e-mail.

57. Reprinted in Bruce Robert's "It's a Long Old Lane Ain't Got No End," *Blues & Rhythm,* May 1997, 5.

58. "See That My Grave Is Kept Clean," transcribed by the author from *Blind Lemon Jefferson: King of the Country Blues,* Yazoo Records, 1069, 1984.

59. James, interview.

BLIND BLAKE

1. Paramount Records ad for "Dry Bone Shuffle," *The Afro-American* (Baltimore), May 28, 1927.

2. Jorma Kaukonen, interview with the author, September 9, 1989.

3. Ry Cooder, interview with the author, February 25, 1990.

4. *The Paramount Book of Blues* (Port Washington, Wis.: New York Recording Laboratories, 1927), 15. This page is reproduced in *78 Quarterly* 1, no. 5 (1990): 14.

5. Transcribed from scans of the original Paramount Records ads that appeared in Jas Obrecht's "The King of Ragtime Blues: Blind Blake & His 'Famous Piano-Sounding Guitar,'" *Guitar Player,* October 1995: "Bad Feeling Blues," 42; "Rumblin' & Ramblin' Boa Constrictor Blues," 40; "Wabash Rag," 43.

6. "Papa Charlie and Blind Blake Talk about It—Part 1," transcribed by the author from *Blind Blake: Complete Recorded Works,* vol. 4, *August 1929 to June 1932,* Document Records, DOCD-5027, 2000.

7. Steve Calt and Woody Mann, liner notes for *Blind Blake: Ragtime Guitar's Foremost Fingerpicker,* Yazoo Records, 1068, 1984.

8. Gayle Dean Wardlow, interview with the author, January 30, 1992.

9. Stefan Grossman, interview with the author, February 22, 1992.

10. Kaukonen, interview.

11. Robert M. W. Dixon, John Godrich, and Howard Rye, *Blues & Gospel Records, 1890–1943,* 4th ed. (New York: Oxford University Press, 1997), 76, 1054, 740.

12. Wardlow, interview.

13. Samuel Charters, *Sweet as the Showers of Rain: The Blues Makers, Part II* (repr., New York: Da Capo, 1977), 144.

14. Dixon, Godrich, and Rye, *Blues & Gospel Records, 1890–1943,* 79.

15. Ishmon Bracey, interview with Gayle Dean Wardlow, transcription mailed to the author in 1989.

16. "Fightin' the Jug," transcribed by the author from *Blind Blake: Complete Recorded Works,* vol. 3, *May 1928 to August 1929,* Document Records, DOCD-5026, 2000.

17. "Hastings St.," transcribed by the author from *Blind Blake: Complete Recorded Works,* vol. 3.

18. John Lee Hooker, interview with the author, December 29, 1992.

19. Grossman, interview.

20.   Irene Scruggs, "Itching Heel," transcribed by the author from *Blind Blake: Complete Recorded Works,* vol. 4.

21.   Cooder, interview.

22.   Alex van der Tuuk, e-mail correspondence with the author, October 20, 2014.

23.   John Tefteller, e-mail correspondence with the author, November 22, 2013.

24.   Alex van der Tuuk, Bob Eagle, Rob Ford, Eric LeBlanc, and Angela Mack, "In Search of Blind Blake: Arthur Blake's Death Certificate Unearthed," *Blues & Rhythm,* no. 263: 8–10.

25.   "Poker Woman Blues," transcribed by the author from *Blind Blake: All the Published Sides,* disc D, Richmond, Chicago 1929, JSP Records, JSP7714, 2003.

BLIND WILLIE McTELL

1.   In an e-mail correspondence with the author on October 27, 2014, David Evans wrote, "McTell was very likely born in 1901. Michael Gray makes a pretty convincing case, based on documents that were not available earlier. McTell himself evidently thought he was born in 1898."

2.   "Monologue on Life as Maker of Records," transcribed by the author from *Blind Willie McTell: The Complete Library of Congress Recordings,* RST Records, BDCD-6001, 1990.

3.   "Just As Well Get Ready, You Got to Die," transcribed by the author from *Blind Willie McTell: The Complete Library of Congress Recordings.*

4.   David Evans, "Kate McTell, Part 2," *Blues Unlimited,* no. 126 (1977): 13. Details of McTell's life were revealed by Kate McTell in her lengthy 1975 and 1976 interviews with Anne Evans, Cheryl Thurber, and David Evans, which first appeared in *Blues Unlimited,* nos. 125, 126, and 127.

5.   David Evans, liner notes for *Atlanta Blues 1933: A Collection of Previously Unreleased Recordings by Blind Willie McTell, Curley Weaver, and Buddy Moss,* John Edwards Memorial Foundation, JEMF-106, 1979, 8.

6.   David Fulmer, "Blind Willie McTell: Atlanta's 12-String Minstrel for All Seasons," *Blues Access,* Fall 1992, 31.

7.   Blind Willie McTell, "Monologue on Himself," *Blind Willie McTell: The Complete Library of Congress Recordings.*

8.   David Evans, "Kate McTell, Part 1," *Blues Unlimited,* no. 125 (1977): 6.

9.   Ibid., 7.

10.   Evans, "Kate McTell, Part 2," 10.

11.   Peter B. Lowry, letter to the author, September 16, 2002.

12.   Transcribed by the author from McTell, "Monologue on Himself."

13.   Evans, liner notes for *Atlanta Blues 1933,* 13.

14.   Dick Spottswood, "When the Wolf Knocked on Victor's Door," *78 Quarterly* 1, no. 5 (1990): 64–77.

15.   Ibid.

16.   David Evans, liner notes for *The Definitive Blind Willie McTell,* Columbia/Legacy, C2K 53234, 1994, 15.

17.   Robert M. W. Dixon, John Godrich, and Howard Rye, *Blues & Gospel Records, 1890–1943,* 4th ed. (New York: Oxford University Press, 1997), 591–92.

18.   These details of McTell's life are from Kate McTell's 1975 and 1976 interviews with Anne Evans, Cheryl Thurber, and David Evans, which first appeared in *Blues Unlimited,* nos. 125, 126, and 127.

19.   Evans, "Kate McTell, Part 1," 6.

20.   Ibid., 11.

21.   Ibid., 6.

22.   Evans, "Kate McTell, Part 2," 12.

23.   Kate McTell quoted in Evans, liner notes for *Atlanta Blues 1933,* 16.

24.   As described by Kate McTell in Evans, "Kate McTell, Part 1," 7.

25.   Lowry, letter.

26.   Evans, "Kate McTell, Part 2," 11.

27.   "I Got to Cross the River of Jordan," transcribed by the author from *Blind Willie McTell: The Complete Library of Congress Recordings.*

28.   "Amazing Grace," transcribed by the author from *Blind Willie McTell: The Complete Library of Congress Recordings.*

29.   McTell, "Monologue on Accidents," transcribed by the author from *Blind Willie McTell: The Complete Library of Congress Recordings.*

30.   Mike Leadbitter, Leslie Fancourt, and Paul Pelletier, *Blues Records, 1943–1970,* vol. 2 (London: Record Information Services, 1994), 198.

31.   Ahmet Ertegun, letter to David Fulmer, August 27, 1991.

32.   Steve Hoffman, message sent via Facebook, October 10, 2013.

33.   Evans, "Kate McTell, Part 1," 10.

34.   Details of McTell's burial wishes and tombstone reported by Kate McTell in Evans, "Kate McTell, Part 1," 10.

BLIND WILLIE JOHNSON

1.   Jas Obrecht, liner notes, Blind Willie Johnson, *Dark Was the Night,* Columbia, CD CK 65516, 1998.

2.   Alan Di Perna, "Jack White: Jack the Ripper," *Guitar World,* August 2007, 78.

3.   Ry Cooder, interview with the author, February 25, 1990.

4.   Texas Department of Health, Bureau of Vital Statistics, Standard Certificate of Death, County of Jefferson, City of Beaumont, 40295.

5.   Draft card reprinted in "Further Draft Card Blues," *Living Blues,* February 2008, 6.

6.   Samuel B. Charters, *The Country Blues* (repr., New York: Da Capo, 1975), 156.

7.   Undated promotional brochure entitled *Marlin,* from the author's collection. The brochure's use of right-facing swastikas as decorative dividers suggests that it was published before the Nazi party appropriated the symbol in 1933.

8.   Charters, *The Country Blues.*

9.   Ibid., 157.

10.   Liner notes for *Blind Willie Johnson: 1927-1930, Edited with an Introduction by Samuel Charters,* RBF Records, RBF 10, 1965.

11.   Charters, *The Country Blues,* 157.

12.   Michael Corcoran, "Retracing the Life of a Texas Music Icon," *Austin American-Statesman,* September 28, 2003. This excellent article is available online as "He Left a Massive Impact on the Blues, but Little Is Known about Blind Willie Johnson," http://www.austin360.com.

13.   Stephen Calt's liner notes for Blind Willie Johnson's *Praise God I'm Satisfied* LP, Yazoo Records, 1058, 2013.

14.   Samuel Charters's CD booklet for *The Complete Blind Willie Johnson,* Columbia/Legacy, C2K 52835, 1993, 12.

15.   Ibid., 13.

16.   Robert M. W. Dixon, John Godrich, and Howard Rye, *Blues & Gospel Records, 1890-1943,* 4th ed. (New York: Oxford University Press, 1997), xxviii.

17.   Ibid.

18.   The original Columbia Records ad is reprinted in Francis Davis's *The History of the Blues* (New York: Hyperion, 1995), 119.

19.   Charters, CD booklet for *The Complete Blind Willie Johnson,* 12–13.

20.   Edward Abbe Niles, "Ballads, Songs, and Snatches," *Bookman,* June 1928, 422–24. Quoted in Mark A. Humphrey's "Holy Blues: The Gospel Tradition," in *Nothing but the Blues,* ed. Lawrence Cohn (New York: Abbeville Press, 1993), 119.

21.   Cooder, interview.

22.   Ibid.

23.   Country Joe McDonald, interview with the author, August 16, 1978.

24.   Charters, CD booklet for *The Complete Blind Willie Johnson,* 22.

25.   Cooder, interview.

26.   Charters, CD booklet for *The Complete Blind Willie Johnson,* 24.

27.   Ibid., 25.

28.   Robert Dixon and John Godrich, *Recording the Blues* (New York: Stein and Day, 1970), 65.

29.   *Texas: A Guide to the Lone Star State Compiled by Workers of the Writers' Program of the Work Projects Administration in the State of Texas* (New York: Hastings House, 1940), 194.

30.   Charters, *The Country Blues,* 164.

31.   Corcoran, "Retracing the Life of a Texas Music Icon."

32.   Charters, CD booklet for *The Complete Blind Willie Johnson,* 16.

33.   Ibid.

34.   Texas Department of Health, Standard Certificate of Death.

35.   Pops Staples, interview with the author, May 11, 1992.

LONNIE JOHNSON

1.   Ry Cooder, interview with the author, February 25, 1990.

2.   "Love Is a Song (Your Love Is Gold)," transcribed by the author from *Lonnie Johnson: Complete Recorded Works, 1925–1937,* vol. 7, *11 February 1931 to 12 August 1932,* Document Records, DOCD-5069, 1996.

3.   Johnny Shines, interview with the author, January 23, 1989.

4.   Gayle Dean Wardlow, interview with the author, 1989.

5.   B.B. King, interview with Billy Gibbons and Jas Obrecht, April 9, 1991.

6.   B.B. King with David Ritz, *Blues All around Me: The Autobiography of B.B. King* (New York: Avon Books, 1996), 23.

7.   John Lee Hooker, interview with the author, April 15, 1992.

8.   Lonnie Johnson, interview with Moses Asch, transcribed by the

author from "The Entire Family Was Musicians," Lonnie Johnson, *The Complete Folkways Recordings,* Folkways Records, SFW40067, 1993.

9.   Ibid.

10.   Pete Welding and Toby Byron, eds., *Bluesland: Portraits of Twelve Major American Blues Masters* (New York: Penguin Books, 1991), 42.

11.   Pops Foster as told to Tom Stoddard, *The Autobiography of Pops Foster, New Orleans Jazzman* (Berkeley: University of California Press, 1973), 92.

12.   Lonnie Johnson, interview with Paul Oliver, July 17, 1960. Transcribed by the author from an audio copy of the original recording provided by the Paul Oliver Collection of African American Music and Related Traditions (Gloucester). Used with Paul Oliver's permission.

13.   Ibid. An edited version of this passage appears in Paul Oliver's *Conversation with the Blues* (New York: Horizon Press, 1965), 79.

14.   Dean Alger, *The Original Guitar Hero and the Power of Music: The Legendary Lonnie Johnson, Music, and Civil Rights* (Denton: University of North Texas Press), 52.

15.   Johnson, interview with Oliver.

16.   Transcribed by the author from a tape recording of outtakes from the Moses Asch interview for Johnson, *The Complete Folkways Recordings.* Tape courtesy Dean Alger.

17.   Johnson, interview with Asch.

18.   Ibid.

19.   "Mr. Johnson's Blues," transcribed by the author from *Lonnie Johnson: Complete Recorded Works, 1925-1932,* vol. 1, *4 November 1925 to 13 August 1926,* Document Records, DOCD-5063, 1994.

20.   Albertson quoted in Welding and Byron, *Bluesland,* 43-44.

21.   *Chicago Defender* ad, June 12, 1926; this was reproduced in *Living Blues,* Spring 1982, 21.

22.   Johnson, interview with Oliver.

23.   Victoria Spivey, "Blues Is My Business" column, *Record Research,* no. 106 (July 1970): 9.

24.   Johnson, interview with Oliver.

25.   Ibid.

26.   "Mean Old Bedbug Blues," transcribed by the author from *Lonnie Johnson: Complete Recorded Works, 1925-1932,* vol. 2, *13 August 1926 to 12 August 1927,* Document Records, DOCD-5064, 1994.

27.   "Fickle Mama Blues," transcribed by the author from *Lonnie Johnson: Complete Recorded Works,* vol. 2.

28.   "Roaming Rambler Blues," transcribed by the author from *Lonnie Johnson: Complete Recorded Works,* vol. 2.

29.   "St. Louis Cyclone Blues," transcribed by the author from *Lonnie Johnson: Complete Recorded Works, 1925-1932,* vol. 3, *3 October 1927 to 28 February 1928,* Document Records, DOCD-5065, 1994.

30.   Tony Russell, "The Guitar Breaks Through," in *Masters of Jazz Guitar: The Story of the Players and Their Music,* ed. Charles Alexander (London: Balafon Books, 1999), 7.

31.   Robert M. W. Dixon, John Godrich, and Howard Rye, *Blues & Gospel Records, 1890-1943,* 4th ed. (New York: Oxford University Press, 1997), 460.

32.   "Kansas City Blues," transcribed by the author from *Lonnie Johnson: Complete Recorded Works,* vol. 3.

33.   Transcribed from the ad reproduced in Thom Carlyle Loubet's "Jazzin' the Blues: The Life and Music of Lonnie Johnson" (senior thesis, Music Department and American Studies Program, Wesleyan University, 1996), fig. 5.

34.   Jeff Todd Titon, *Early Downhome Blues: A Musical and Cultural Analysis,* 2nd ed. (Chapel Hill: University of North Carolina Press, 1994), 219, 221.

35.   Ibid., 221-22.

36.   Loubet, "Jazzin' the Blues," 54.

37.   Ibid, 58.

38.   Dan Lambert, "From Blues to Jazz Guitar," in *The Guitar in Jazz: An Anthology,* ed. James Sallis (Lincoln: University of Nebraska Press, 1996), 38, 40.

39.   "Broken Levee Blues," transcribed by the author from *Lonnie Johnson: Complete Recorded Works, 1925-1932,* vol. 4, *9 March 1928 to 8 May 1929,* Document Records, DOCD-5066, 1994.

40.   Johnson, interview with Oliver.

41.   Johnson, interview with Asch.

42.   Samuel B. Charters, *The Country Blues* (repr. New York: Da Capo, 1975), 78-79.

43.   Johnson, interview with Oliver.

44.   Loubet, "Jazzin' the Blues," fig. 4.

45. "When You Fall for Some One That's Not Your Own," transcribed by the author from *Lonnie Johnson: Complete Recorded Works,* vol. 4.

46. "George Van Eps on Eddie Lang," as told to Jim Ferguson, *Guitar Player,* August 1983, 85.

47. Lambert, "From Blues to Jazz Guitar," 40–41.

48. Loubet, "Jazzin' the Blues," fig. 6.

49. Larry Cohn, interview with the author, July 1993.

50. Nat Shapiro and Nat Hentoff, eds., *Hear Me Talkin' to Ya: The Story of Jazz by the Men Who Made It* (New York: Rinehart, 1955), 271–72.

51. Chris Albertson, *Bessie* (London: Abacus, 1975), 149.

52. Jim O'Neal and Amy van Singel, "Living Blues Interview: Georgia Tom Dorsey," *Living Blues,* March–April 1975, 28.

53. Loubet, "Jazzin' the Blues," fig. 9.

54. Charters, *The Country Blues,* 74.

55. Johnson, interview with Oliver.

56. Oliver, *Conversation with the Blues,* 148.

57. "Man Killing Broad," transcribed by the author from *Lonnie Johnson: Complete 1937 to June 1947 Recordings,* vol. 1, *8 November 1937 to 22 May 1940,* Blues Document, BDCD-6024, 2001.

58. "It Ain't What You Usta Be," transcribed by the author from *Lonnie Johnson: Complete 1937 to June 1947 Recordings,* vol. 1.

59. "Mr. Johnson's Swing," transcribed by the author from *Lonnie Johnson: Complete 1937 to June 1947 Recordings,* vol. 1.

60. Ibid.

61. Bob Yelin, "Jazz Guitar Wouldn't Be the Same without George Barnes," *Guitar Player,* February 1975, 26.

62. Mike Newton, e-mail correspondence with the author, May 17, 2013.

63. Johnson, interview with Asch.

64. Jerry Ransohoff, "Record Firm Here Smashes Jim Crow," *Cincinnati Post,* March 21, 1949, 6.

65. King with Ritz, *Blues All around Me,* 24.

66. "Happy New Year Darling," transcribed by the author from Lonnie Johnson's *Me and My Crazy Self,* Charly CD 266, 1992.

67. Jim O'Neal, e-mail correspondence with the author, July 12, 2014.

68. Steven C. Tracy, *Going to Cincinnati: A History of the Blues in the Queen City* (Urbana: University of Illinois Press, 1993), 137.

69. Ibid.

70. Mike Leadbitter and Neil Slavin, *Blues Records, 1943–1970: A Selective Discography,* vol. 1 (London: Record Information Services, 1987), 714.

71. Albertson quoted in Welding and Byron, *Bluesland,* 40.

72. Ibid., 40.

73. Ibid, 40–41.

74. Chris Albertson, e-mail correspondence with the author, January 28, 2014.

75. Dan Deluca, "Tribute CD Brings Lonnie Johnson Back to Life," *Philadelphia Inquirer,* April 1, 2008.

76. Ibid.

77. Spivey, "Blues Is My Business," 9.

78. Ibid.

79. King with Ritz, *Blues All around Me,* 23.

80. John Hammond, interview with the author, July 25, 1990.

81. Stefan Grossman, *Masters of Country Blues Guitar Featuring Lonnie Johnson* (Miami: CPP Belwin, 1993), 3–4.

82. Albertson quoted in Welding and Byron, *Bluesland,* 48.

83. Transcribed from scan of original *New York Times* blurb, November 23, 1961; e-mailed by Chris Albertson to the author, January 28, 2014.

84. Spivey, "Blues Is My Business," 9.

85. Valerie Wilmer, "Lonnie Johnson," *Jazz Monthly,* December 1963, 5.

86. Ibid, 7.

87. McHarg quoted in John Goddard, "The Final Years of Lonnie Johnson," *Blues Access,* Winter 1998, 33–34.

88. Hooker, interview.

89. McHarg quoted in Goddard, "The Final Years of Lonnie Johnson," 35.

90. Cohn, interview.

91. "Falling Rain Blues," transcribed by the author from Johnson, *The Complete Folkways Recordings.*

92. Flohill quoted in Goddard, "The Final Years of Lonnie Johnson," 36.

93. McHarg quoted in Goddard, "The Final Years of Lonnie Johnson," 36.

94. Spivey, "Blues Is My Business," 9.

MISSISSIPPI JOHN HURT

1. Larry Cohn, liner notes for Mississippi John Hurt's *Avalon Blues: The Complete 1928 OKeh Recordings,* Columbia/Legacy, CK 64986, 1996, 6.

2. "Avalon Blues," transcribed by the author from *Mississippi John Hurt: 1928 Sessions,* Yazoo Records, 1065, 1990.

3. This information appears in Stefan Grossman's "'Scrapin' the Heart and Knockin' Them Back': A Classic Interview with the Legendary Mississippi John Hurt," *Sing Out!* 39, no. 4 (February/March/April 1995): 54. It was derived from an interview that Tom Hoskins conducted with Hurt at the Ontario Place in Washington, D.C., on October 13, 1963.

4. This information appears in the original eighty-nine-page unpublished transcription of Tom Hoskins's October 13, 1963 interview. A complete Xerox copy of this document was sent to the author by Nick Perls in 1986.

5. Philip R. Radcliffe, *Mississippi John Hurt: His Life, His Times, His Blues* (Jackson: University Press of Mississippi, 2011), 18.

6. Grossman, "'Scrapin' the Heart and Knockin' Them Back,'" 54.

7. Stefan Grossman, *The Music of Mississippi John Hurt* (Miami: CPP/Belwin, 1993), 6.

8. "Lazy Blues," transcribed by the author from *The Immortal Mississippi John Hurt,* Vanguard, SVRL 19005.

9. Cohn, liner notes.

10. Hoskins, transcription, 3–7.

11. Ibid., 47.

12. Ibid., 44–45.

13. Watson quoted in Grossman, "'Scrapin' the Heart and Knockin' Them Back,'" 57.

14. "Little John," unbylined article, *Time,* September 27, 1963, 64.

15. Ibid.

16. Mike Leadbitter and Neil Slaven, *Blues Records, 1943–1970: A Selective Discography,* vol. 1 (London: Record Information Services, 1987), 198.

17. Dick Waterman, interview with the author, September 7, 2012.

18. Rory Block, interview with the author, August 1983.

19. Sky quoted in Grossman, "'Scrapin' the Heart and Knockin' Them Back,'" 55.

20. Van Ronk quoted in Grossman, "'Scrapin' the Heart and Knockin' Them Back,'" 55.

21. Dick Spottswood, interview with the author, June 1995.

22. "Little John," 83.

23. Robert Shelton, "City Lends an Ear to Country Singer," *New York Times,* January 16, 1964, 28.

24. Stefan Grossman, interview with the author, June 1, 1978.

25. Waterman, interview.

26. Watson quoted in Grossman, "'Scrapin' the Heart and Knockin' Them Back.'"
27. Sebastian quoted in Grossman, "'Scrapin' the Heart and Knockin' Them Back,'" 53.
28. Grossman, interview.
29. Ibid.
30. Ibid.
31. Scott Baretta, review of Philip R. Ratcliffe's *Mississippi John Hurt: His Life, His Times, His Blues,* in *Living Blues,* December 2011, 65.

TAMPA RED
1. Ry Cooder, interview with the author, February 25, 1990.
2. James Litke, "When Tampa Sang the Blues," *Farmington Daily Times,* April 23, 1981, 20.
3. Jim O'Neal, liner notes for *Tampa Red: The Guitar Wizard,* RCA Bluebird, AXM2-5501, 1975.
4. Ibid.
5. Mark Humphrey, "Johnny Shines: A Living Legacy of Delta Blues," *Frets,* November 1979, 37.
6. Big Bill Broonzy, *Big Bill Blues: William Broonzy's Story as Told to Yannick Bruynoghe* (London: Cassell, 1955), 90.
7. Robert M. W. Dixon, John Godrich, and Howard Rye, *Blues & Gospel Records, 1890–1943,* 4th ed. (New York: Oxford University Press, 1997), 741.
8. Ibid., 881.
9. "It's Tight Like That," transcribed by the author from *Tampa Red: Complete Recorded Works,* vol. 1, *May 1928 to 12 January 1929,* Document Records, DOCD-5073, 2001.
10. Jim O'Neal and Amy van Singel, "Living Blues Interview: Georgia Tom Dorsey," *Living Blues,* March–April 1975, 25.
11. Williams quoted in Mark A. Humphrey's "Bright Lights, Big City," in *Nothing but the Blues,* ed. Lawrence Cohn (New York: Abbeville Press, 1993), 165.
12. Handy quoted in Stephen Calt, *Barrelhouse Words: A Blues Dialect Dictionary* (Urbana: University of Illinois Press, 2009), xiv.
13. O'Neal and van Singel, "Living Blues Interview: Georgia Tom Dorsey," 25.
14. Ibid., 26.

15. This quote is taken from a Xerox copy of Jim O'Neal and Amy van Singel's original typewritten transcription titled "Thomas A. Dorsey Interview 11/27/74 Chicago," 50.

16. O'Neal and van Singel, "Living Blues Interview: Georgia Tom Dorsey," 27.

17. Ibid., 28.

18. O'Neal and van Singel, transcription, 26.

19. O'Neal, liner notes for *Tampa Red: The Guitar Wizard.*

20. Ibid.

21. Blind John Davis, interview with the author, June 13, 1979.

22. Ibid.

23. Broonzy, *Big Bill Blues,* 90.

Index

JAS OBRECHT

A MUSIC JOURNALIST since the 1970s, Jas Obrecht was a staff editor for *Guitar Player* magazine for twenty years. His writings on blues music have been in *Rolling Stone, Living Blues, Blues Revue,* and many other publications. He is author of *Blues Guitar: The Men Who Made the Music* and *Rollin' and Tumblin': The Postwar Blues Guitarists* and coauthor, with James "Al" Hendrix, of *My Son Jimi.*